Jakli McDowell.
B. Theol 1.

A Christian Vision for State Education

A CHRISTIAN VISION
∞ **FOR STATE EDUCATION** ∞

Reflections on the Theology

of Education

—

TREVOR COOLING

First published in Great Britain 1994
Society for Promoting Christian Knowledge
Holy Trinity Church
Marylebone Road
London NW1 4DU

British Library Cataloguing-in-Publication Data
A catalogue record for this book is available from the
British Library

ISBN 0–281–04758–8

Typeset by Wilmaset Ltd, Birkenhead, Wirral
Printed in Great Britain by
Biddles Ltd, Guildford and King's Lynn

To Charles Martin,
whose Christian commitment, intellectual vigour,
sheer hard work, and sacrificial giving
have been a source of inspiration to so many
seeking to think as Christians about education,
and to my colleagues at Stapleford House
who are seeking to make his vision a reality.

Contents

Preface

TWENTY YEARS MAY seem a long time to take to write a book of this length. However, as I read my words through once more, it seems as though I have only scratched the surface of the issues that are raised in the attempt to relate theology and education.

This book began in 1973 when, as a student teacher, I was first challenged about the place my Christian faith should play in my work in the classroom. I was then, and still am now, an Evangelical Christian. I was active in the Christian Union at Cambridge and, in my final year, chaired the committee that planned a University-wide mission. As I prepared to enter teaching, I did so in the firm belief that the gospel of Jesus Christ is good news for all people. Part of my vocation as a Christian teacher was to share that with my pupils.

I soon became very aware that such evangelistic zeal was considered inappropriate, anti-educational, even dangerous by many educationists. There seemed to be a polarization between the professionals, who regarded themselves as neutral and objective, and those like myself who were at best guilty of confessionalism and at worst of indoctrination. As a teacher, I often felt that I was a covert operator, required to work under one set of obligations while secretly clinging to different obligations derived from my personal Christian theology. I desperately felt the need for a resolution of this tension. As an Evangelical Christian teacher, I needed to make an honest man of myself; I needed to create a genuine harmony between my work as a teacher and my faith as a Christian. I was not happy to be in education simply to engage in guerilla warfare against the dominant educational philosophy. This book is the fruit of my attempts to resolve these dilemmas.

The book has taken shape through a number of different experiences. My teacher training introduced me to the issues. It also gave me the privilege of meeting and working with John Shortt, who has shared my intellectual and spiritual journey in struggling with the issues since then. My nine years of teaching religious education in county schools brought me face to face with the practicalities of the classroom—not least the need to respect the genuine differences of opinion that there are in matters of religion. My work with the Association of Christian Teachers, particularly with religious education teachers, has underlined the destructiveness of the polarization between Christian commitment and education that has dominated British thinking since the 1970s. Most important of all has been my work for an MA degree at King's College, London, and subsequently, for a Ph.D at Birmingham University, when I was able to write at length on this topic. The fact that these events have spanned twenty years has meant that I have known, too, the fascinating experience of watching how both Evangelical Christians and educationists have modified their positions in response to the debates.

I am very aware of the limited nature of this study. My concern is for the way in which religion is dealt with in what are sometimes called State schools. Here the need is to develop a curriculum that meets the aspirations of many different faith communities. This cannot be neutral, but I suggest it can be secular without being specifically anti-Christian, or, more generally, anti-religious. However, those looking for the development of a distinctive Christian theory of education for the Church or Christian schools will not find it here. This is another, albeit important, task that I leave to others with the necessary experience. Even so, the issues raised by this limited study are enormous. To tackle them has meant venturing into the philosophy of knowledge, many areas of theology, political theory on the role of the State, social theory on the nature of society and debates as to the aims of education. As such, I believe the study of this limited area of educational theory offers a wonderful case study in applied theology.

Trevor Cooling
July, 1993

Acknowledgements

THERE ARE MANY people who have contributed, some of them unwittingly, to the appearance of this book. My employers, the Association of Christian Teachers, allowed me the freedom to pursue my studies. The many people who have debated the issues with me on courses at Stapleford House have stretched my thinking. David Cook, Ieuan Lloyd, Deborah Pitt, John Shortt, and Elmer Thiessen have read and commented most helpfully on various drafts. Ruth Cooper and Paul Truby have struggled with me in producing a typescript. I am also indebted to the All Saints Educational Trust, The Hockerill Educational Foundation, the St Gabriel's Trust and the Whitefield Institute for the financial support they have given me for my studies.

There are a further four people to whom I owe a particular debt. The work of three of them—Brian Hill, John Hull, and Michael Grimmitt—has been a particular inspiration to me over the years. I could not have written this book without the benefit of their scholarship and their personal encouragement in taking my thinking forward. In making criticisms of their ideas, I am well aware that I am building on foundations laid by far greater minds than my own. I hope that they will take this book as a tribute to their work and as thanks for their inspiration.

The fourth person I would like to thank is my wife Margaret. Without her encouragement, this project would have been abandoned long ago. Our marriage has been a privilege and fulfilment. To enjoy sharing a working life as well is a much appreciated bonus.

This book is offered with the prayer that it will help all of us involved in secular education to be true to our own personal commitments in a way that is honest, responsible and of benefit to our students and colleagues, irrespective of their own religious persuasions.

Introduction

IN THIS BOOK, I argue that there is a way of relating theology and education that is acceptable both to those professionally engaged in secular education and to members of faith communities. It may be helpful if I summarize the main points of the argument as they will be developed throughout the book.

In Part I, I argue that the currently influential, liberal approach has failed because it defines educationally acceptable religious belief, one that is both rational and tolerant of other faiths, in terms of a particular theology, which I call *radical Christian liberalism*. This strongly emphasizes individual freedom of choice, is suspicious of absolute commitment, and is antagonistic to religious nurture. Furthermore, it endorses *relativism* as the way forward for building good relations among members of different religions. Finally, I argue that this liberal approach is characterized by a tendency to treat religious language as *instrumental*, even *subjective*, rather than as making absolute statements about reality. In Chapter 4, I noted how this theology has been accorded an authority over and above other types of theology because it is deemed to support educational principles which are themselves taken to be rational and objective. My major criticism of this approach is that it is a violation of the *pluralist principle*, namely that secular schools should not impose a particular form of religion on their students. The liberal approach is not, then, fair in its treatment of the religions because it discriminates in favour of *radical theology*, and against *more traditional forms* of religious commitment. Western liberal values are imposed under the guise of claiming that educational principles are rooted in rationality, and therefore, are independent of religious belief.

In Part II, I seek to break the impasse by suggesting a way in which concern for rational believing can go hand-in-hand with the notion of fairness as embodied in the pluralist principle. This means redefining the notion of rational belief in ways that recognize the role of commitment, but also require the believers to accept some responsibility for ensuring that their beliefs are true by examining evidence, and engaging in debate with others. I describe this attitude as truth that listens, or, more technically, as *critical realism*. This embodies the idea of an open commitment that seeks to ensure its propositions match reality as closely as possible.

In addition, I also argue that our attitude towards State schooling has to change. It cannot be treated as being independent of controversial belief, as though it has some superior status over religion. Rather, I argue that each person's educational vision will depend on their basic beliefs. In this situation, State education, an enterprise which has to meet the needs of all citizens, can only have limited goals in relation to religion. This is because it is essentially a coalition among people who have very different ultimate commitments, but who recognize the importance of providing an education in religion that enables people to live together as fellow citizens in our modern plural society. It is, therefore, a very different exercise, I will argue a less significant one, from religious nurture that does not have to cope with the restraints experienced by State schools.

In Part III, I address the question of whether *Evangelical Christian theology* can work with the view of schooling I describe. I concede that some Christians will not be able to do this, because they do not have the theological resources to encourage them to value working alongside, and learning from, those whom they differ from. They cannot, therefore, endorse the need for fairness in the treatment of religion in State schools. A detailed case study of Brian Hill's writings shows how easy it is to go the other way, and let secular educational thought dictate terms of theology. However, I suggest there is a third option, the *transformationalist*, which allows Evangelical Christians to endorse many of the ideals of secular education, in particular, the importance of pursuing a vision for the common good in partnership with those from whom we may fundamentally disagree, but in a way, which maintains the primacy of theology. A survey of several modern Evangelical writers shows that the tradition does offer the theological resources needed for this task.

I cannot speak for other theological traditions. I can only offer my reflections as an Evangelical Christian in the hope that they may provide some inspiration for my compatriots in other theological traditions who are wrestling with the challenges that religious pluralism poses for modern State schools. Of one thing I am sure. We ignore the issue at our peril.

❧ PART I ❧

—

Insecure Foundations
for
Religious Education

CHAPTER ONE

Introducing the Debate

Introduction

THERE IS A conversation I had a few years ago that has had a lasting influence on my thinking ever since. I was in debate with a friend about the relationship between education and Christian belief. His position can be summed up as follows:

> Education is essentially concerned with the pursuit of truth. Christianity is true. So education ought to be based on Christianity.

These comments take me back to my early encounters with the philosophy of science as a second year undergraduate. The lecturer began the course by telling us that if we were not confused by the time he had finished his series of lectures, then we simply had not understood the subject. The difficulty with my friend's simple solution was that he had apparently never understood the complexity of the questions that are raised when we seek to bring education, truth, and Christian theology into alliance. It seems that, as far as he was concerned, there simply were no dilemmas to face.

It is, of course, possible to become totally paralysed by complexity. John Habgood, also reminiscing on his days as a student, said that one of his lecturers was someone who knew so much, and knew so many objections to anything that could be said, that there was a great danger that saying anything at all with confidence became impossible. However, the strength of this particular person was that, at the end of his lecture, one would be exposed to, as the Archbishop put it, 'five minutes of pure gold', when his own commitments were put on the table.[1] The authority for those last five minutes was, of course, derived from the previous fifty, when his grasp of the complexities of the subject matter was revealed. This was no trite commitment.

The problem with education, and particularly where it touches religion, is that teachers are so easily overwhelmed by the complexity of the issues that they never find those five minutes of pure gold, which should be the goal of any defensible process of critical reflection. The result is an education with no religious vision and with no commitment—a most dangerous commodity in a world where any hope for our future lies in the possibility of principled action.

The challenge for Christians involved in education is, then, to find the narrow way that lies, often disguised, between the two extremes of certainty and paralysis when it comes to religious values. The danger of the former is that it becomes totalitarian and of the latter that it gives no basis for a vision on which to build life. Since the mid twentieth century, the consensus in British education has swung dramatically between these two extremes. Well into the 1960s, most teachers never doubted their role in passing on the Christian faith as the moral and religious foundation for young people's lives. This certainty evaporated in their almost Damascus Road awakening to the existence of religious and moral pluralism that took place during the late 1960s and beyond. *Indoctrination* became the cardinal sin of education and *neutrality* its guiding principle—a message relentlessly drummed home in teacher training. In more recent times, growing dissatisfaction with the values vacuum generated by this approach has led to a resurgence of certainty about values. On the one hand, there has been the politically influential movement to reassert the Christian heritage of Britain. One legacy of this is legislation in England and Wales that requires school worship and religious education to be mainly Christian.[2] On the other hand, there has been a professionally influential movement that has mounted an attack on more traditional forms of religious belief—but more of this later.

Many years of working alongside Christian teachers has convinced me that this swinging pendulum between certainty and paralysis is taking a serious toll; it is yet one more contributory factor to the high stress levels experienced in modern schools. There is a desperate need to find a way for Christians—indeed, for all people of religious commitment—to be at peace with their personal religious vision while also being true to the complexity of the educational demands made on them. This means finding a way of thinking theologically about education that remains faithful both to the truth as understood within the Christian faith, and to the educational responsibilities laid on those working in modern schools. This book is an attempt to achieve this end, or, at least, to find the gateway to the narrow path.

What to do with Pluralism

For Christians, perhaps one of the most pressing theological questions in the modern world is how to respond to the fact of religious pluralism.[3] However, the idea that it is the task of education to reflect this religious plurality is increasingly being disputed. The fact that adherents to religions other than Christianity comprise only a very small minority of the total British population is often cited as an argument against what is perceived to have been an exaggerated emphasis on multifaith religious education in schools. Surveys show that eighty per cent of people today regard themselves as Christians. This 'pop vox' view is cited as clearly showing the need for an education system based on the transmission of Christian beliefs.

However, to adopt this view is to forget that the concept of religious pluralism has very little to do with the percentage make-up of the population and everything to do with the fact that religion is inherently controversial. Even within the Christian Church, there is a wide-ranging pluralism. This is easily demonstrated by asking a variety of Christians what they believe about the nature of Christ, or what they understand to be the significance of the Resurrection, or of the Eucharist, or what they believe about the role of women in the Church—to take just a few examples. So, it simply does not help to claim that Britain is a Christian country. Even if this were true, pluralism and controversy in the religious domain would still be facts of life. Schools have a responsibility to help young people come to terms with them.

A pressing task facing modern education must, therefore, be to accommodate religious pluralism within common schools[4] without fragmenting their educational vision. In 1985, the Swann Report, *Education For All*, coined the phrase 'diversity within unity' as the appropriate goal to aim for. To reach this, Swann argued that it would be necessary:

> to achieve a balance between . . . the maintenance and active support of the essential elements of the cultures and lifestyles

of all ethnic groups within it . . . and the acceptance by all groups of a set of shared values distinctive of society as a whole. (page 6)

The Swann Committee recommended that a *phenomenological approach*[5] should form the basis of the shared values that underpin an educational approach to religion. In this, students and teachers alike are expected to bracket out, or distance themselves from, their own commitment to religious truth in the cause of an objective study of religion, aimed at promoting mutual understanding. So, objectivity becomes the basis of the shared values. However, a major criticism made of the Report was that it is simply not possible to bracket out religious aspirations in the way the phenomenological style of teaching takes for granted (Islamic Academy, 1985; Jones, 1986). They are, to put it simply, too fundamental for that. Unity cannot be achieved by asking people to privatize beliefs that they hold as universal and non-negotiable. If schools are to deal successfully with religious pluralism, in other words, in a way that is not divisive, requiring religious passion to be left at the school gate will not work. Such an approach does not prepare children for dealing with controversy; it simply ignores it.

An Influential Alternative

In a stimulating book published in 1990, Chris Arthur points to another way forward, which is based on making what I will call *liberal educational values*[6] the framework for cohesion within diversity. In his Introduction, he recalls his horror at being handed a tract that claimed that the Zeebrugge disaster was 'God's message to the nation'. He saw this as symptomatic of a religious sickness, superstition got up as religion, that pointed to a massive failure in religious education.

According to Arthur, such tracts are like miners' canaries, giving warnings that we ignore at our peril. In his view, this sickness has reached epidemic proportions and is as much in evidence in the ignorant rejection of all things religious as in the resurgence of literal religious fundamentalism. The teacher's responsibility is to combat such attitudes.

John Hull, who is Professor of Religious Education at Birmingham University, has made an extensive analysis of this notion of religious sickness in his book *What Prevents Christian Adults From Learning* (1985a). In this book, he seeks to identify those forms of belief that make learning in the religious domain difficult. He sees the origin of the problem as lying in the pressures that are brought to bear on believers by the confusions of life in the modern world. In particular, he identifies the crucial significance of the experience of what he calls 'bafflement', as religious believers encounter ideas that challenge the very heart of their belief structures. This is a common experience today because the increasing pluralization and secularization of society relativizes and privatizes beliefs previously seen as absolute. In other areas of life, such bafflement is accommodated by a process of 'cognitive bargaining', a learning process whereby changes are made in our belief system in response to new ideas. For example, the fact that people can sail round the world means that we no longer believe the earth is flat. However, such is the powerful nature of religion as a source of personal meaning and identity that, according to Hull, for many people, the stakes are simply too high for such bargaining to be possible. The response is to retreat into the safety of orthodoxy to protect one's beliefs against decreasing plausibility, rather than to respond to the challenge of learning generated by living in the modern world. Hull calls this retreat 'ideological enclosure'.

The danger of this response is that it drives underground the fact that we cannot match our religious beliefs with our experience of the world. In other words, we suppress the fact that we are baffled. This puts religion into the romantic categories of childhood, that world of fairy-tales we would like to retain but that we know in our heart of hearts has no place in the modern world. The driving motivation for accepting enclosure is a psychological need for certainty, and a desire to retreat from the process of modifying our beliefs that has to happen in cognitive bargaining. The ideological community receives and protects those who are heavily laden, and insulates them from the demands of modernity. This is a serious *learning sickness*, and those who suffer from it Hull calls 'stage defenders',[7] those who are unwilling to progress in their faith development, preferring to remain with their childhood experience of religion.

As far as Hull is concerned, the consequences of this sickness are very dangerous. On the one hand, if the process of protection is successful, the result is ideological hardening and enclosure. Elsewhere (1992) he calls this type of believing 'religionism', a form of tribalism that engenders attitudes of rejection and exclusion arising out of a fear of contamination by other forms of religion. The prognosis for the future of the plural society is very poor if this condition is widespread in religious communities, as difference is seen as something to defend oneself against, rather than an opportunity for creative learning. For Hull, the fact that religionism is alive and well was evident from the attitudes that were displayed by opponents of multi-faith religious education in the debates that preceded the passing of the 1988 Education Act for England and Wales.[8]

On the other hand, the danger is that individuals will be unable to sustain the tension that develops as they seek to maintain a public life in the modern world and a private life of religious ideological enclosure. They increasingly find that, 'in a changing world, an unchanging theology soon becomes irrelevant' (Hull, 1984, page 208). The result can be a total loss of faith, as individuals find themselves having 'grown out of' religious belief under the pressures of persisting bafflement. Like many of the old clothes kept in the wardrobe because of a reluctance to dispose of them, faith simply no longer fits.

Religious learning sickness, therefore, drives a person into one of two unpleasant states: either intolerance, based on the need to be certain; or scepticism, as the attempt to hang on to religious meanings becomes ever less plausible. Hull shares Chris Arthur's belief that a major responsibility of schools is to combat this sickness. He calls this 'anti-religionist education'.

For these writers it is not, therefore, enough for schools simply to encourage tolerant attitudes towards other religions through an objective study of religion. What is necessary, is a sustained attack on ideological enclosure. They are insistent that this is not an assault on religious identity as such, but an attack on religious belief that is held in an irrational, totalitarian manner, and refuses to face up to the challenges of being a religious learner. In their view, therefore, religious education can be seen as a programme of religious health education, which has as its aim the combatting of learning sickness or religionism. It promotes unity by encouraging an approach to religion that all reasonable people can accept. At the same time, it honours diversity, as all genuine religions have, within them, the resources to be reasonable. Learning sickness is something that no self-respecting religion will want to encourage.

What Hull has spelt out in explicit terms is implicit in the writing of many other people on religious education. In particular, there is, I suggest, a widespread concern in the literature with two main 'symptoms' of this sickness. The first is the inability to hold faith in a rational manner. Irrational faith cannot accommodate our advancing knowledge of the world. It is threatened by change. The second is an intolerant dogmatism, which is expressed in the fear of, and unwillingness to accept, differences of religious opinion. A detailed consideration of these 'symptoms' will occupy the next two chapters. However, before turning to this, it is important to note a major anxiety that has been expressed about the approach of Hull and others.

A Major Anxiety

Central to the learning sickness model is the assumption that it is possible to reach a non-controversial understanding as to what constitutes a 'healthy' approach to religion. As it is based on the principles of rationality, this can then, it is argued, form the basis of education for all in the common school. In an important book published in 1989, Edward Hulmes has questioned whether this is, in fact, the case. His main point is that our view of what counts as rational belief will be determined by what our religious beliefs are in the first place. His conclusion is that, in educational circles, a western analytical view is currently taken for granted as the normative view of religious rationality in the multicultural situation.

Hulmes builds his criticisms of this situation on the widely accepted principle that education in common schools should be non-confessional—in other words, not based on any particular faith position. He argues that the modern liberal view is no different to other monocultural responses. It, too, has 'an ideological confessional character of its own' (1989, page 18). As far as he is concerned, education can only truly respect the fact of religious pluralism if the liberal view of the status of religious knowledge is open to challenge by other perspectives. In his opinion, this is not currently the case and the result is that 'the concept of pluralism is simply ignored' (1988, page 86). The concern for diversity is sacrificed to a false notion of unity based on liberal ideals, which, in the extreme, amounts to little more than a euphemism for secularism.

Muslims have been making this same point for some time. They have argued that modern approaches amount to the rationalizing of a cultural dominance by the secularist, anti-religious majority (Islamic Academy, 1985, pages 4–5).

The aim of education, from an Islamic point of view, is the realization of total submission to God. In its approach to religion, the philosophy influential in common schools is seen as being in direct conflict with this Islamic view. So, Syed Ali Ashraf has suggested that the liberal—he calls it secular—basis of common schooling in Britain should be replaced by one that is built on the widely shared 'Judaeo-Christian-Islamic beliefs in God, man's accountability to God and after life' (1988, page 71). In his opinion, such a framework would be acceptable to all the main faith groups in the country and would therefore promote diversity within unity as it is based on values that really are shared. This is in contrast to the imposed secularist framework that is based on a view of religious rationality antagonistic to many forms of religious belief, not just Islam.

Christians, too, have challenged the basis of modern educa-tion on the grounds that it propagates an anti-religious theory of knowledge. The writings of Lesslie Newbigin (1986, 1989, 1991) have been particularly influential. He is concerned about 'the division of human life into public and private and the separation of fact and value' (1986, page 34). The public world of facts is, he argues, treated as independent of faith commitment. In his view, this represents a particular and controversial 'plausibility struc-ture', or way of viewing the significance of religion in modern life. Imposing this cannot be a basis for diversity within unity.

Newbigin's view is that the role of the Christian is to proclaim the gospel faith as public truth for all. To accommodate the Christian message to the modern, secular plausibility structure is to domesticate it in such a way that its inherent message is denied. Rather, a biblical plausibility structure provides us with a set of lenses or concepts through which we see the world (1989, page 38) that is totally different to that employed in the liberal approach to education. He rejects the notion that it is immedi-ately obvious that 'the modern historical consciousness of western twentieth-century intellectuals provides us with a van-tage point which can displace the one provided by the Christian story' (1989, page 160). In contrast, to be faithful to the kingdom of God, Christians should continue to claim the high ground of public truth in schools over and against this secular model.

To many in modern Britain, such views may seem to be sectarian and no basis for an ethical, or even practical, approach to education for all in our plural society. However, if the aspiration to achieve diversity within unity is to be realistic, they cannot be dismissed simply as the views of the lunatic fringe. The call for Islamic education to be available for Muslim children within the maintained sector is politically potent. Within Christian circles, the perceived anti-Christian bias of what has been dubbed the 'multifaith mishmash' approach to religious education, lies behind the influential demand[9] that religious education should be predominantly Christian.

It is important to remember that the concern is not with the teaching of other religions as such—few of the critics deny that these have a place in the classroom—but with 'a multifaith relativism' (Burn and Hart, 1988, page 4), or the adoption of a 'multifaith creed' (page 8), which is seen as secularist in intention.[10] The important debate, therefore, is about the philosophical and theological framework within which education is to operate. The objection is to the attempt to prescribe a liberal view of religious belief as the basis for common schooling. Therefore, there is a clash here between the widely accepted views of certain educationalists and religious minorities that are having a considerable influence on educational legislation. The basis of the clash is a fundamental disagreement over how religious belief and education are to be related. Clearly, any viable approach to achieving diversity within unity in schools cannot ignore such a fundamental conflict.

In the next four chapters, I will examine this charge that liberal education is currently propagating a secularist belief system that is antagonistic to traditional forms of religious belief and that it thereby contradicts its own claim to be non-confessional and sympathetic to pluralism. My conclusion will be that the evidence supports the criticisms made by Hulmes and others. However, contrary to some, I still want to argue that aspiring to the goal of diversity within unity in the context of the non-confessional, common school is both possible and worth while.

This will entail a reappraisal of liberal values in order to develop a set of shared educational values that can form a basis for cohesion without compromising the reality of religious diversity. I do this by offering a redefinition of what it means to be reasonable in religion that is not, I trust, profoundly offensive to traditional forms of religious belief, and a redefinition of liberal education that accords with modern aspirations. I attempt this reappraisal in Part II. Finally, in Part III, I will seek to show how Christians from the Evangelical tradition, one that is often perceived as only supporting a specifically Christian form of education, can positively endorse these reinterpreted, liberal values. In doing this, my hope is to offer a methodology that will be of use to other religious traditions.

CHAPTER TWO

Whose Rationality?

Introduction

PROBABLY THE MOST influential feature of educational philosophy over the last forty years has been the liberal ideal of
rational autonomy, critical rationality, or critical openness, as it
is variously called. The Australian author Brian Crittenden has
given a helpful description of this as follows:

> In our cultural tradition, individual responsibility and self-
> direction are upheld as characteristics of a mature human life.
> The valuing of self-direction is closely linked with the open
> expression and criticism of opinions, the testing of beliefs in
> relation to the broad range of relevant experience, the critical
> search for adequate explanations and reasons; in summary,
> the practice of open rationality. (1988, page 100)

This tradition has radically changed the way that teachers think
about the place of religion in education. No longer is it seen to be
adequate for schools to seek Christian commitment in their
pupils. Open, critical rationality requires something more.

Such vague aspirations are not enough, however. We need to
have a clearer picture of the results of applying open critical
rationality to religious belief if we are to assess the charge that
this liberal, educational ideal is antagonistic to more traditional
forms of religion. I shall suggest that it is because it entails an
exaggerated emphasis on scepticism and individualism that is
threatening to traditional religious ways of life.

Religious Scepticism as an Educational Outcome

In the liberal view, the antithesis of education is indoctrination.
The educational ideal is that a student should never hold an

unjustified belief. In contrast, indoctrination has taken place when a belief 'is maintained without due regard to the relevant evidence and argument' (Callan, 1985, page 115).

In the British context, Paul Hirst has probably been the most influential advocate of this thesis.[1] For Hirst, it is fundamentally important that education develops in individuals the propensity to hold religious beliefs in a fashion appropriate to their rational status. This is very different to the uncritical adherence to beliefs and practices that he sees in many religions. The role of true education is to discourage such uncritical adherence. He contrasts this with approaches to teaching that transmit the concepts, beliefs and values of a particular tradition as a content to be accepted on the authority of that tradition. As far as he is concerned these are inadequate.

As a young student teacher, I had the privilege of being trained by Paul Hirst. It was a most stimulating experience, but I also found it profoundly disturbing. Hirst was, and still is, insistent that the intention of his approach to education is not to induce a general state of critical scepticism or doubt (1985, page 13). However, I felt that my Christian faith was most definitely under threat and that I was being asked to be sceptical about things that were fundamentally important to me. I could, however, not identify why I felt like this. I began to meet with two or three Christian friends to discuss these anxieties. We became convinced that a major part of our difficulties lay with Hirst's distinction between religious belief and knowledge. Twenty years on, I am still convinced that this is the problem.

Hirst's thesis is that there are various forms of knowledge. These are objective, being independent of culture and belief. They are characterized by public criteria for testing truth, which are distinctive to each of the forms. Testing scientific, mathematical, or moral truth is, therefore, the same the world over. The conclusions arrived at as a result of these tests constitute a body of true propositions that are universal. The forms, therefore, define the knowledge that rational endeavour has uncovered. The role of education is to initiate students into these public and universal modes of thought and, in particular, to their critical apparatus for testing truth. In Hirst's earlier writings, religion was regarded as having a legitimate claim to be one of these forms of knowledge, but later he changes his mind. Thus, he writes:

if in fact, as seems to be the case at present, there are no agreed public tests whereby true and false can be distinguished in religious claims, then we can hardly claim that we have a domain of religious knowledge and truth. (1974a, page 181)

The logic of Hirst's position is that this marks out religious beliefs as having a different status from the publicly agreed forms of knowledge. This has profound implications for education. As Hirst himself expresses it:

Somehow the distinction must be got over so that pupils grasp the objective necessity for accepting the conclusions of reason and the voluntary commitment that alone is appropriate in the face of the claim's of one's [religious] faith. (1981, page 92)

Religion cannot, therefore, be accorded the public or objective status that would make it central to an education based on rational principles. Rather, it must be satisfied with a private, voluntary role. This is in marked contrast to the universal knowledge discovered through the exercise of reason.

This distinction is of fundamental importance in Hirst's argument. He is going far beyond the recognition that religious belief is a controversial matter with no implied judgement as to its rationality. He is, rather, advancing an argument for what we might call its 'radically contestable nature'. This means that 'the best evidence and argument available for it is weak or we do not even have clearly defensible criteria for what would count as evidence or argument in its favour' (Callan, 1989, page 271). So, we find writers assuming that religious beliefs are inferior because we do not hold them in the same way that we hold scientific beliefs (for example, Burtonwood, 1986, page 137). We should, therefore, be sceptical about them in a way that we do not have to be with the forms of knowledge. Religious belief has a doubtful status, which means it cannot have the public authority accorded to the forms of knowledge governed by the principles of rationality alone.[2]

Such arguments have serious implications for our attitude to the religious way of life. If religion really *does* have such a dubious rational status, it is difficult to see how anyone can have the confidence in it that is required if wholehearted worship is to be possible. The Canadian philosopher Eamonn Callan argues that this tension between the maintenance of religious forms of life and the critical, rational principle is not taken seriously enough in philosophy of education (1989). Certainly, if Hirst is correct, it would appear that the contrast between knowledge and religious belief must engender scepticism in our attitude to the latter. It is hard to see how the person educated on Hirstian principles can sing 'I know that my Redeemer liveth' with any integrity. Therefore, it seems that education may be inextricably linked with promulgating doubt in relation to religion. For, if education is only to transmit beliefs according to their rational status, then religion must be transmitted as radically contestable. This is in marked contrast to other areas, such as science.

Hirst, however, does not face up to the implications of the distinctions he makes between religion and the forms of knowledge. As far as he is concerned, rational societies will still have their churches. Indeed, to use his words, the experiences they offer 'are amongst the most valued amongst men' (1974b, page 90). Not valued enough, however, to be allowed a significant role in education. It seems that Hirst is prepared to sanction people believing and practising in private what is publicly unjustifiable, as long as they do this in a rational way. Unfortunately it is unclear exactly what *is* the rational way to hold a belief having this private status. It is difficult to see how it could include the committed action characteristic of the religious way of life. Martyrs do not die for beliefs that they regard as having a rationally dubious status compared to other knowledge, they die for the truth.

In his book *The Culture Concept in Educational Studies*, Neil Burtonwood argues that education should adopt this sceptical view of religion.[3] Unlike Hirst, however, he does acknowledge that this means undermining absolute religious commitment as education will then be about 'seeking rational explanations, while religion is ultimately about faith' (page 135). The learner will, therefore, have to adapt to the fact that 'nothing is certain any more' (page 140), learn to tolerate doubt, and develop an ambivalence to religious commitment. This is the price that religion will have to pay if it is to relate to education. Burtonwood can see no reason why this should not be acceptable in a rational, open society. It is now clear to me why I felt so threatened as a Christian student training for teaching.

The Cult of the Individual

There is a second, worrying consequence of this attempt to draw such a sharp distinction between the forms of knowledge and religious belief. According to Hirst, to be rational is to be initiated into the former so that we become committed to using their public criteria for testing truth. The role of education based on rational principles is to promote this commitment. With religion there are, however, no such public criteria for testing truth. In this case, the role of education is to encourage pupils to choose for themselves, as it is irrational to accept contestable beliefs on someone else's authority. Religious commitment is, then, to be treated as a private affair, a matter of personal choice of beliefs that do not have the necessary rational basis for them to be part of the framework of public life. The objective forms of knowledge are uncontroversial and certain; in contrast, religious belief is controversial and uncertain. To fail to make this distinction and to treat religious belief as though it had the authority of a public form of knowledge are clear symptoms of learning sickness. In religion, to be rational is to be autonomous, to choose for oneself.

The increasing religious pluralism of modern society means that it is simply no longer possible to be ignorant of the fact that religious options exist. For Burtonwood and others like him, pluralism, therefore, is to be welcomed because it is a challenge to the 'irrational' idea that particular groups have the right to pass on their beliefs, unquestioned, to their children. So, Burtonwood argues that 'the ultimate goal of the educational process must be autonomy . . . and this includes autonomy with respect to roots' (1986, page 160). To seek to be free from choice is to enter a pathological, irrational state. Individualism, therefore, is a consequence of this approach to religion and rationality. Yet, traditionally, religious communities pass on their beliefs from generation to generation.

Both Hirst and Burtonwood come from what can be called the objectivist tradition. They hold that knowledge is ultimately external to the knower and is present in certain public disciplines to be discovered, mastered and learned. Michael Grimmitt, another influential English writer on religious education, takes a different view.[4] He argues that knowledge is 'a social construct, socially related and socially relative' (page 18). This conception, in which knowledge is never absolute, but only reflects agreements that are shared by a group of people with a common culture or ideology, is commonly described as relativism.

However, even though his view of knowledge is fundamentally different from that of both Hirst and Burtonwood, Grimmitt still reaches the same conclusions as to the importance of individual choice. In order to understand his emphasis on autonomy, one has to appreciate the pivotal role that the concept of humanization plays in his view of education. Central to his account is the idea that it is possible to identify certain characteristics that define what it means to be human. He describes these as givens that are 'universal or necessary truths of an anthropological kind contingent upon the human condition as it happens to be or more simply facts about human life which are constant, irrespective of culture or ideology' (page 69).

Grimmitt discusses a number of these givens, but, for him, the most important is the attempt to give some meaning to our existence. We do this by holding beliefs about the nature of reality. Indeed, we have no choice but to interpret our experience by holding beliefs and values. We simply cannot function in the world without doing this. For Grimmitt, a critically important point about these beliefs is that they shape the sort of persons we become. I will be a very different person if I believe that all life is sacred than if I believe in the superiority of the Aryan master race. It is an inescapable fact of the human condition that we are products of what we believe. Grimmitt regards this as an uncontroversial statement about the human condition.

According to Grimmitt, these shaping beliefs have two sources. First, there are those beliefs that are held unconsciously and into which we have been socialized as a result of our cultural history. We cannot learn in a vacuum; our human condition makes us interdependent with others. However, this is only part of the story as each person is unique, each has a personal history. This ability to develop a personal vision is an expression of the freedom that distinguishes the human from the animal. 'Men and women are more than the sum of all the biological, social, cultural and ideological influences which shape them, and they themselves can play a part in shaping the person that emerges from the context of such influences' (page 79). For Grimmitt, playing this part is a reflection of another distinctively human capacity—the ability to choose the beliefs that shape us as persons. Combining these facts, our freedom to choose beliefs, and the shaping effects that our beliefs have on our personal future, adds up to our having responsibility for the people we are becoming. The more we take this responsibility seriously, the more fully human we are.

So, he writes that: 'Playing this part—participating in shaping one's own self and taking responsibility for the person one is becoming—is an expression of the human capacity to choose and is thus a mark of being human' (page 79). In his analysis, primacy is given to this personal biography, which enables one gradually to break free from one's cultural history. The influence of a community on one, by contrast, seems to be viewed as a prison, cramping the process of humanization if it remains unchallenged by other ways of viewing the world. It is important, therefore, to 'enrich children's stocks of personal histories' (page 99) so as to minimize the danger that adolescents are given an identity by others rather than choosing one for themselves (page 207). So, he speaks approvingly of pupils 'rolling their own' (page 208) when it comes to stances for living.

This brings us to one defining characteristic of Grimmitt's work, namely that he sees choosing as an authenticating experience, having value in its own right, irrespective of the content of what is chosen. Religion, seemingly, becomes true as it is chosen by an individual, but cannot be regarded as true in some objective, pre-existent sense outside of the realm of human experience. Freedom to choose, therefore, is a right and responsibility that education should seek to maximize, if it is to fulfil its proper function of promoting humanization. Pluralism is important in this process as it acts as a catalyst, opening up the possibility of more and more choice, and challenging the adequacy of our previously unquestioned beliefs.

This emphasis on the importance of individual choice leads us back full circle to our first theme of scepticism. For Grimmitt, an important feature of this process of choosing is that it always entails risk as it can only be based in hope, not knowledge in any absolute sense. So, he writes:

The human struggle for meaning has produced many alternative views of what it means to be human, but no single definitive answer which can in some way be proved to be true by reference to incontrovertible evidence or empirically verified fact. . . . The empirical carpet runs out from beneath this question and we find ourselves choosing between beliefs about the human. (page 73)

Grimmitt concludes from this that we can no longer be certain of anything except that relativity and uncertainty are facts of life (page 27), because there are no objective criteria available for choosing in the religious domain (page 225). Religious choices, therefore, must always be provisional as they take us beyond the limits of reliable knowledge. It would be quite wrong for anybody to think that they have found the final truth. Doubt, it seems, is a virtue. To cease to choose is to allow ourselves to be dehumanized. Continuing uncertainty and individual choice, therefore, are inextricably linked in a rational approach to religious belief.

Implications for a View of Christian Nurture

Grimmitt, Hirst, and Burtonwood, therefore, seem to share a view of education which entails that it promotes a sceptical attitude to religious beliefs, places a high value on free, autonomous choice, and treats such choices as a purely personal matter. This puts religious belief in a very different category to other forms of belief (for example, the scientific and moral) that have a public authority not enjoyed by religion. To combat learning sickness, then, is to encourage children to make their own religious choices, while, at the same time, ensuring that they are aware of the uncertain nature of these choices, and of the need to hold them in a tentative fashion. All in all, there is a strong suggestion here that absolute commitment to a particular religion, or identification with a particular religious community by children is irrational and should be discouraged by education. In other words, it seems as though education is, by definition, antagonistic to religious nurture.

Certainly, if learning sickness is the serious matter it is believed to be by these writers, it surely follows that we should combat it in whatever way we can. As one writer expressed it, 'if religion is epistemologically unsound in school, it is unsound anywhere' (Lloyd, 1986, page 143). However, it is not always made clear in the educational literature what should happen when the values of education and those of religious nurture come into conflict with each other. The democratic values espoused by most commentators make them reluctant to inter-fere in the privacy of a person's home life, despite its perceived deficient nature and its anti-educational, anti-liberal conse-quences. However, as Eamonn Callan says, 'it is surely rash to assume that there is some approach to teaching about religion which poses no great threat to the maintenance of religious forms of life while fully honouring the rational–critical principle' (1988, page 184). So, the tension remains unresolved.

The general ambivalent attitude to this problem that exists in works on education can be illustrated by extracts from Paul Hirst's writings. He, apparently, is quite happy that 'private' institutions should engage in nurture (1974b, page 90). He is even prepared to allow that schools can engage in the nurturing activity of catechesis, as long as this complements education by promoting a rational attitude (1981, page 90; McLaughlin, 1992a, pages 3–5), but this is to ignore the problem that the doubt engendered by his educational philosophy is inimical to much nurture and to most, if not all, religious practice, especially worship. If, as Hirst suggests, separate faith commu-nity schools are likely to be less than rational in their approach (1985, page 16), it surely follows that the same will be true of the other faith-nurturing activities of these communities. The experience of many school pupils under a Hirstian regime will be to find that the approach to religion encouraged by the home and the faith community is in direct conflict with the critical, rational approach advocated in school. They find themselves facing a stark choice between rationality and faith. It is simply dishonest for education to maintain that it is valuing the contribution of religious nurture, when the education experienced by children is actually destructive of it.

Michael Grimmitt has attempted to resolve this by arguing that nurture and education are compatible activities, but appro-priate to different contexts. In his article 'When Is Commitment a Problem In Religious Education?' (1981), he contrasts the aims and assumptions of the two processes, arguing that there is a great gulf between them. His conclusion seems to be, although this is not specified, that both are valid, but that a clear distinction must be made between their roles and the assumptions that underpin them. They are, therefore, entirely different processes (page 46) that serve different contexts (page 47). Certainly, there is no suggestion that nurture is inferior or even harmful in this article, and this is true of the very few mentions the subject gets in his major book *Religious Education and Human Development* (1987a pages 39–40, 79–80, and 259).

However, the tension in his thought on this issue is revealed in a brief passage in his earlier book *What Can I Do in RE?* (1978). Here, he describes the expectation of people going to church 'either to be initiated into Christian faith and belief or to have their already accepted Christian commitment sustained and deepened' (page 22), as being entirely appropriate. However, there is a significant, but undeveloped, caveat that this is an adult activity. In the next paragraph, he goes on to argue that it is morally and educationally questionable to instruct children in schools with the intention of moving them towards a religious commitment. The state school, he says, unlike the Church, has the responsibility of educating the child in religious understanding. Here, their respective, presumably complementary, roles are clear. The Church instructs, schools educate. If this is the case, though, why has he, in just the paragraph before, been at such pains to suggest that the confessional activity of the Church is only appropriate as an *adult* activity? This seems to imply that instructing children in Christianity is immoral in the Church as well as in school. Such a tantalizing aside hints at the idea that Grimmitt believes that children should not be given a religious upbringing by a faith community, or, presumably, their parents.

Certainly, from the logic of his argument regarding humanization, it can be assumed that he thinks that the religious nurture of children is an unhelpful activity. The argument is simply this: choosing beliefs for oneself has ultimate value because it promotes humanization. As he expresses it, the 'meaning-making potential of human beings is increased in proportion to their capacity to choose between beliefs' (page 82). According to his definitions, nurture must, because it takes place within one tradition (page 259), be anti-humanistic as it does not promote choice. In his view, the pluralized context of modern secular education is able to promote humanization in a way that the monolithic structure of the faith community cannot. Education and nurture, therefore, must conflict as to promote free choice is to undermine the nurturing aspiration of leading a child to Christian, or any other particular religious commitment.

A good example of this conflict between the attitudes of education and those of religious nurture is when Grimmitt discusses religious pluralism. He argues that 'the ideological stance of most religions to pluralism . . . is antithetical to the ideological stance towards pluralism which is part of a liberal conception of education' (page 245). This assertion is supported by research carried out by some of his students, which suggests that to become 'open' to the 'truth' of other traditions is to 'place oneself, from the point of view of the particular religious tradition, outside [religious] faith itself' (page 175). Therefore, he notes that, for most pupils with an Asian background, especially for Muslims, education will be in conflict with the religious understanding valued in their homes (page 179). This will, of course, also be true for those children coming from more conservative Christian traditions. Grimmitt is anxious that education should attribute worth to these pupils' religious commitments (page 179), but gives no clear guidance as to how this is to be achieved when there is such a profound conflict between the aims of nurture within these communities and the aims of education. It seems as though religious community life is being treated as little more than a licensed insanity.

Other writers[5] have pursued the logic of these arguments more rigorously and justify combatting the influence of parental or faith community nurture on the grounds that it is incompatible with the educational goal of promoting rational belief. There are two justifications put forward for this (Callan, 1985). First, they argue that the child's right to self-determination is threatened by a religious upbringing. Children should not be victims of their backgrounds, suffering the limitations of their parents. Nurture is problematic because it entails unjustified intervention in the belief-forming processes of children by reducing their capacity for choice.

Second, such upbringing is thought to result in people holding religious beliefs in an unshakeable manner that does not give serious attention to their rationally contestable status. Religion generates strong emotional attachments and is a significant source of personal identity for many people. Linked to the fact that beliefs formed in the early years tend to stick (Gardner,

1988, pages 94–8), this makes religious beliefs powerful determining and shaping forces in the believer's life. For these
writers, nurture is problematic because it does not foster critical
openness. As John Hull puts it, 'in a society where everything is
to be examined, how can a process in which some things are not
to be examined escape inferior status?' (1984, pages 210–11).

Some Concluding Remarks

Thus, it seems that there is an agreement among some influential
writers that religious belief is not fully rational. They see it as
important that education should challenge the certainties that
tend to take root in children's religious thinking. In all the cases
we have examined, this is linked with an absolute value being
placed on what is variously referred to as self-determination
(Callan, 1985), the right to choice (Grimmitt, 1987a), liberal
autonomy (Gardner, 1989), or, more popularly, children
becoming 'free-thinking metaphysical speculators' (Gardner,
1988, page 97). The justification for this emphasis on autonomy
is not always clear, however.

John Shortt (1986) has argued that, in discussions of autonomy, two different conceptions of it are present, namely rationality and authenticity. Shortt claims that, among educationists,
openness to criticism is the most widely held understanding of
the rationality component. However, in their discussions of
religion, none of these writers have succeeded in defining
objective criteria for truth testing, as are believed to exist in
other areas of knowledge, which would give clear guidelines
for selecting between religions when opening one's beliefs to
criticism. Therefore, it seems that, in religion, unlike, for
example, science and morals, openness to criticism provides
minimal guidance as to the conclusions that can be reached on
the basis of rationality.

It is not surprising, therefore, to find that the emphasis for the
writers that have been the subject of this chapter is on authenticity. They want children to become authentic, self-directed
people, as opposed to inauthentic, other-directed people. To be
a product of one's background is educational anathema. From
this, it is concluded that the more potential for choice one has,
and the more free choices one actively makes, the more
authentic a person one is.

There are, here, clear hints of existentialism. However, this, of itself, will not account for the emphasis on autonomy by writers like Hirst and Burtonwood. For them, the value placed on the act of choosing is based on the assumption that liberty is a foundational principle of morality, and that any infringement of it is, prima facie, in need of justification.[6] Any intervention in the life of another person, of which education and nurture are both examples, must always be justified. On rational grounds, it is possible to justify intervening in the development of children's thinking in domains where there are clear objective means for testing truth. There cannot be freedom for children to choose in matters that are rationally non-debatable. In religion, such grounds are not considered to exist and, therefore, intervention is never justified. At the point where rationality does not provide the equipment for adjudication, the value placed on liberty demands that people choose for themselves in the light of careful consideration of the available alternatives. Such choice is a private matter, in the sense of being the concern of the individual, and should not be predetermined, even by those in one's family. It is this liberal belief in the right of the individual to liberty that seems to underlie much of the concern that children should not be shaped by others when it comes to religious beliefs. It is a right that overrides any rights parents might have to pass on their faith to their children.

My intention, so far, has been to describe rather than criticize this liberal view of education. However, two brief criticisms will be alluded to now, because of their significance later in the book.

First, the picture of religious belief that it paints has little to do with the way in which most believers hold their faith. As D. Z. Phillips says, the embarrassment for the liberal view is that 'it does not do justice to the primary language of faith. Strong belief is not tentative or hypothetical. Believers do not pray to a God who probably exists' (1988, page xii). This is why, despite attempts to argue otherwise, education based on the views I have been describing cannot give a positive rationale for the nurturing activity of the faith community. In seeking to describe religion, it destroys much of it. The account is, essentially, prescribing a rationalist ideal rather than describing the reality.

Second, the problematic nature of this liberal position is underlined by its objection to the notion of religious upbringing. The conclusion of the arguments put forward would seem to be that family life for religious people is simply not possible. It appears that, in order to be moral, parents who are committed to the value of a life of worship are never to involve their children in this life. The values that underpin their own existence cannot form the basis of their family life. Besides being an assault on parental rights, it is an attack on the concept of upbringing altogether. If beliefs acquired early in life tend to stick, and the ideal is rational autonomous choice as adults, it appears that the best policy might be to abolish all upbringing and thereby avoid children acquiring beliefs in an irrational fashion! Alternatively, perhaps what is being suggested is that the task of upbringing should be delegated to common schools as it seems that they, in contrast to the parental home, are the places where rational and objective educational values are maintained.

The liberal objection to religious upbringing ignores other fundamental issues, including the privileges and responsibilities accepted in the process of procreation, the necessary close personal relationships of family life, and the fact that parents, more than anyone else, bear the consequences of the upbringing of their children. All these factors support the right of parents to have a considerable say in the upbringing of their children.[7] It also ignores important developments in the theory of knowledge, which are discussed in Chapter 6.

CHAPTER THREE

The Desire for Tolerance

Introduction

IN THE LAST chapter, it was argued that the liberal view of education, with its emphasis on preventing learning sickness, promotes a particular view of what it means to hold a religious belief rationally. There is, however, a second important feature associated with writers who are concerned about learning sickness—namely the adoption of a particular theology of religious pluralism. In this chapter, we shall examine this theology, and unpack its implications for education.

A pressing concern for theologians is the need to find a practical solution to the problem of religious conflict. Many people believe that education has an important role to play in enabling those who disagree in the religious domain to learn to live together in the modern, plural societies of the global village. For example, in the national model syllabuses for England (School Curriculum and Assessment Authority, 1994), the national guidelines for Scotland (Scottish Office Education Department, 1992) and a consultative document produced by the Association of RE Advisers and Inspectors (AREAI, 1989), one of the stated aims of religious education is to encourage pupils to respect the right of others to hold beliefs that are different to their own. Education should be providing an alternative to the defensive mentality of the religious tribe. Gordon Kaufmann expresses this aspiration well:

> it is a necessity today for religious and secular communities that differ and disagree to come to a sufficient understanding of each other to enable them to enter into positive dialogue and other interaction, instead of persisting in the sort of separation, distrust and even warfare that may destroy us all. (1987, page 4)

It does not take many hours of watching the television news to appreciate the importance of this concern.

In his analysis of learning sickness, Hull regards the key

challenge for believers confronted by the fact of religious pluralism to be the threat to their religious identity.[1] The 'diseased' response is one that spends time and energy on the defence of one's own belief system on the assumption that it is absolute and that its purity must be maintained. Such attitudes make it impossible to learn from religions different to one's own.

Rubem Alves (1985) came to similar conclusions in his study of one absolutist belief system, which he calls 'Right Doctrine Protestantism'. He sees the key problem as being its obsession with truth. This arises as a result of thinking about doctrine in terms of propositional statements about the nature of reality rather than in terms of their beneficial psychological or sociological effects. The end result is a 'faith seeking certainty' (page 55). According to Alves, such people, who see themselves as guardians of the truth, are bound to be intolerant, particularly when that truth is tied up with the eternal salvation of souls. This type of theology cannot respond to new and pressing demands by promoting right actions (*orthopraxis*); rather, its concern is the maintenance of the old knowledge (*orthodoxy*). Alves sums up his concerns by stating that 'anyone who possesses the truth is condemned to be an inquisitor' (page 203). He would, no doubt, agree with Burtonwood's opinion that there seems to be an empirical link between truth, certainty, and the mentality of Auschwitz (1986, page 109). The threat to peace, therefore, comes from those who seek to distinguish right and wrong in religious doctrine, and pass judgement on the beliefs of others.

For Alves, the educational response must be to help students develop a more creative theology that encourages them to treat the new situation of religious pluralism as fruitful and creative, rather than threatening. In his influential book on religious education, Edwin Cox takes a similar position when discussing the theological commitment of teachers:

> an attachment to one point of view . . . with the corresponding assumption that all other faiths are mistaken and possibly pernicious, will not help the teacher to present fairly and with understanding the other beliefs which the syllabus may prescribe for study. (1983, page 54)

Developing a similar point, John Hull (1985a, pages 36–9, and 1991b) draws on Reinhold Niebuhr's description of three types of religious consciousness found in the modern world: *polythe-*

ism, *henotheism*, and *monotheism*. Henotheists have a single, restricted loyalty that defines their identity and, for them, demarcates truth from falsity. They are inherently tribal in nature, and expend great effort in creating theological justifications for 'distrusting the outside world, hating it, and defeating it by evangelizing it and converting it' (1985a, page 38).

Polytheists are people with divided loyalties for whom there are several different 'gods' that provide meaning in life. Monotheists, however, have broken away from polytheism in that their loyalties are now unified, but have gone beyond henotheism in that they are no longer tribal in their attitudes. Their loyalty is not just to the defence of the focus of their own life, but to that of other people as well.

This analysis enables Hull to define the educational task. It is to enable students to 'move away from divided loyalty [polytheism] and limited and tribalistic loyalty [henotheism] into the true monotheism of universal faith' (1985a, page 38). This offers students a positive way forward as they each contemplate the value of their own faith in the face of the new facts of religious pluralism. According to Hull, the teachers who will be best equipped for this task are those who have themselves found a personal theology that enables them to be committed to divergence (by which he means the educational value of teaching a number of faiths) on religious grounds (Hull, 1980a, and 1982). Such teachers will be exemplars of monotheism.

What, though, are the features of this universal, monotheistic faith? Initially, we can point to two, which are widely assumed to be definitive among writers on religious education.

First, religious doctrines are assumed to have an instrumental rather than a truth-claiming function, such that the 'primacy of orthopraxis over orthodoxy' (Knitter, 1987, page 192) is taken for granted. Orthopraxis is the belief that the role of theology is functional, to promote good actions and attitudes, rather than to maintain purity of abstract doctrine, as is the case with orthodoxy. For example, for Grimmitt, this functional end is the promotion of humanization. If, in order to achieve it, certain previously held doctrines have to be modified, or even jettisoned, then that is the price that has to be paid for theology to fulfil its true function. This is also the rationale for John Hick's objection to the doctrine of the uniqueness of Christ.[2] Abandoning it makes one more tolerant, so it is a welcome change.

Second, it is widely assumed that sound religious education has to be based on some theory of religious relativism (Grimmitt, 1987a, page 107; Hill, 1990b). So, the fact that there clearly are a number of different religions entails the thought that each is seen as a product of a particular background. One's religion, then, is an accident of birth. The general acceptance of relativism is illustrated by the widespread use of the parable of the elephant and several blind men who are each holding different parts of the elephant's body.[3] This is cited as a model of the appropriate educational attitude to other religions. As each blind man has an accurate, but incomplete, grasp of the elephant's anatomy, drawn from his own experience, so each religion has a true, but partial, insight into the nature of God. Many argue that this theological response to pluralism is the only possible basis for the educational values of being sensitive to, and respectful of, other people's views, being tolerant of people who are different from ourselves, being open-minded, and so on.

The difficulty with this theology of pluralism, however, is that it is not compatible with traditional forms of belief that see Christianity as uniquely true. Therefore, it is revisionist, a challenge to traditional theology. As such, it is in need of justification if it is to be the basis of education. Furthermore, we have to ask whether it is true that this approach to other religions is the only one that can underpin values of respect and openness (this will be challenged in Chapter 6). We also have to ask whether the position is as free of difficulties as its exponents claim. An examination of the ideas of two key writers in this field will show that this is not so. John Hick has been chosen because of his influence on theories of religious education. Unfortunately, his ideas undermine the absolute commitment characteristic of religious faith. Joseph Runzo, recognizing that such commitment is essential to the religious way of life, seeks to overcome this difficulty while still maintaining a theory of religious relativism. However, in holding on to the idea of absolute commitment, Runzo is, in the end, forced to let go of his relativism.

John Hick and Religious Pluralism[4]

Hick's starting point is that the absolutist approaches to religious pluralism that have traditionally dominated Christian thinking, and assume the superiority of Christianity, are no longer adequate.[5] He argues that the traditional approaches cannot accommodate the fact that other religions clearly have what he calls 'salvific potency'. In other words, they achieve good outcomes in people's lives. In his view, this demands a new response to pluralism. It cannot come from the a priori arguments of dogmatic theology, but, instead, is based on an inductive argument arrived at as the best explanation of the facts we observe when we examine the various religions. Modern believers (Christians and others) need a theological strategy that encourages a realistic, practical, creative, and positive response to other religions. His alternative, *pluralist theology of religions*, which is an attempt to provide this, has four features that are of significance in this study.

1: RELIGION AS 'SEEING AS'

Hick accepts that the heart of the believer's hope is that one's religious beliefs are true references to reality. He believes, therefore, that any adequate theory of religious belief must respect the everyday use of religious language (1985, pages 16–17; 1989, chapter 11). He seeks to accommodate this reality-describing feature of religious language by arguing that each religious belief is a description made from within the experience of a particular culture (the *phenomenal world*) of that which lies beyond all culture (the *noumenal world*). He calls this noumenal reality the *'Real an sich'*, or the *divine Reality*. So, 'the phenomenal world is the noumenal world as humanly experienced' (1985, page 105). There is only one noumenal reality, but there is a multiplicity of phenomenal worlds, as many as the millions of different human understandings of God that can be found in the world. All religious experience, therefore, is 'seeing as'; there can never be direct apprehension of the 'Real an sich'.

2: RELIGION AS SALVIFIC

For Hick, it is a fact that anyone can observe that something of vital significance is taking place in all the world's religions. They are all salvific in the sense of being centrally concerned with the transformation of the human situation. This may be understood in different ways in the different religions, but Hick's suggestion is 'that these different conceptions of salvation are specifications of what, in a generic formula, is the transformation of human existence from self-centredness to a new orientation, centred in the divine Reality' (1988, page 366).

Although he admits that there is a need for further empirical research, Hick feels that the evidence of history and experience is that no one religion has the monopoly on this process. Therefore, it is a fact that no one religion is salvifically superior.

Hick's position is summarized thus in his own words:

> Pluralism is the view that the great world faiths embody different perceptions and conceptions of, and correspondingly different responses to, the Real or the Ultimate from within the major variant cultural ways of being human and that within each of them the transformation of human experience from self-centredness to reality-centredness is manifestly taking place. (1985, page 36)

The real value of any religion for Hick lies in this instrumental function—the effect it has on the lives of believers—and not on the particular content of its doctrines.

3: THE DANGER OF ABSOLUTISM

Following from his insight that all religions are salvific, Hick is very concerned about religious absolutism, the belief that I am right, and everyone else is wrong, as evidenced in, for example, the dogma that there is no salvation outside of the Christian experience of Christ. He sees such an attitude as validating all sorts of evils.

The attractiveness of absolutism is that it provides a sense of belonging to those others who have also found the truth, thereby fulfilling the natural human need for identity. The danger comes when the legitimate need for corporate self-respect within a particular religion becomes enshrined in formal doctrines as articles of faith, which then become absolutized and non-negotiable. The phenomenal has become confused with the noumenal. In these circumstances, pluralism can only become a threat, and each one of us makes our religion the touchstone by which we judge others.

Hick sees this response as unwarranted if we really face the facts concerning how we came to hold our religious beliefs in the first place. For the vast majority of people, they are simply transmitted from generation to generation. From an absolutist position, whether or not someone is saved seems, therefore, to depend on the geographical location of their site of birth. Hick calls this 'genetic confessionalism'. For him this is a nonsense.

4: CONFLICTS OF DOCTRINE

As we have seen, Hick believes that religious beliefs do point to an independent reality. He is anxious to maintain that there is only *one* reality that *all* the religions describe (1989, page 449). However, this leaves him with the problem of explaining why religions seem to conflict in what they have to say about this one reality. He attempts to tackle this problem of doctrinal conflict as follows.

First, Hick considers reason to be a very limited tool for comparing religious doctrines. So, he says 'I do not think, however, that such a comparison can lead to the conclusion that one set of theories outclasses the rest. . . . Each accordingly accounts for some facts better than others' (1985, page 81). There can be stimulating debate for those who enjoy this sort of thing, but, in the final analysis, reason offers no definitive conclusions.

This leads him to his second conclusion. In principle, he grants that it *is* possible that one belief system may be more accurate than another in describing the 'Real an Sich'. However, he really cannot see that this is of much consequence when the truth we end up with can never be more than speculation. As far as Hick is concerned, doctrinal differences are of no significance when it comes to the subject of salvation; the fact that two religions teach *incompatible* doctrines does not matter when they are *both* salvific. As long as we have only hunches, preferences or inherited convictions, but no secure knowledge, it is not appropriate that religious beliefs should become absolute dogmas. What really matters is their effects in the life of the believer.

Hick's recommendation on conflicting truth claims, therefore, is that we follow the example of the Buddha and refuse to answer undetermined questions. 'Let us then accept that we do not know whether e.g. the universe was created *ex nihilo* nor whether human beings are reincarnated; and further that it is not necessary for salvation to hold a correct opinion on either matter' (1988, page 373).

As we have seen, Hick accepts that religions have a cognitive, truth-claiming component, and that this is essential to religious commitment. However, in his concern to resist absolutism and promote tolerance between religious adherents, he loses sight of this important point. This can be shown in two ways.

On Grading Religions

We have already seen that Hick regards rational criteria as inadequate for grading religions. In his opinion, the moral and spiritual fruits of religions provide a much better basis for judging between them. For him, it is self-evident that the world's religions share a common aspiration to transcend self-centredness in favour of reality-centredness. It is the *degree* to which they fulfil this that should be the measure of the worth of particular religions.

One key characteristic of a reality-centred religion seems to be the denial of absoluteness (with Knitter, 1987, Chapter 2). As far as he is concerned, this is the major reason why the literal understanding of the Christian doctrine of the Incarnation, that God became man, is no longer tenable. So, he writes:

> Thus, whereas understood literally the doctrine of a unique divine incarnation in Christ has divided humanity and has shrunk the image of God to that of the tribal deity of the West, understood mythologically it can continue to draw people to God through Christ without thereby sundering them from the rest of the human family. (1989, page 372)

So, the ability of different religions to describe the 'Real an sich' is judged, in part, by whether or not the doctrines espoused are non-absolutist. Certain doctrines are no longer 'true' because they are inappropriate in the modern, plural context. Therefore, clearly, religious doctrines are judged on an instrumental basis— the degree to which they promote pluralist attitudes. At this point, Hick is departing from his ideal that religious language should be treated in the way ordinary religious believers use it.

Instead, he is proposing that the function of religious beliefs is to achieve certain effects on the believer's feelings, attitudes and actions rather than to describe reality.

Conflicting Truth Claims[7]

We have already seen that Hick is anxious to play down the notion of conflict between truth claims. One strategy he employs to do this is to invoke the notion of *complementarity*, the idea that different religions are equally adequate descriptions of the same reality. To illustrate this, he cites the two descriptions of light as waves and particles (1985, pages 98–9). In the same manner that light can legitimately be described in these two different ways, so the 'Real an sich' can be described in different ways without contradiction. Such descriptions are equally valid accounts of the one reality, rather than one being absolutely right, and the others absolutely wrong.

An illustration of the problem with this approach comes in the seeming contradiction of trying to describe God as both personal *and* impersonal (1985, page 91). This is only plausible if these two descriptions relate to two different aspects of God as he actually is. Complementary descriptions can only be justifiable if the object being described has a complexity that supports these two different perspectives. The parable of the blind men and the elephant (1985, pages 96–7; see page 34) succeeds in communicating its message because the elephant clearly does possess a complexity that enables it to be described in a variety of ways. However, there is the world of difference between saying that the trunk is like a snake, and the legs like a tree trunk, and claiming that the elephant is the size of a mouse, on the one hand, and the size of bulldozer, on the other. Describing God as both personal *and* impersonal has more affinity with the latter than with the former. Complementary descriptions cannot be contradictory.

In order to overcome this difficulty, the concept of mystery is invoked. So, divine Reality is said to be both infinite and ineffable. There can, therefore, never be a cult of the 'Real an sich'. Our phenomenal experiences are, in some sense, caused by an independently existing divine Reality, but that is as far as we can go in talking about the 'Real an sich'; beyond this it is almost entirely unknowable.

The same idea is expressed in the Jain teaching of *anekanta-*

vada that Ken Oldfield (1986, page 178) cited as a sound model for approaching truth claims in religious education:

Maybe it is
Maybe it is not
Maybe it is and is not
Maybe it is indescribable
Maybe it is and is indescribable
Maybe it is not and is indescribable
Maybe it is and is not and is indescribable

However, the outcome of such arguments, for many religious believers, is scepticism, because, as Hick himself points out (1985, page 16), it is exactly the confidence that the God one *believes* in is the God who is actually *there* that is so important to the ordinary believer. What purports to be a *descriptive* account of religion as lived out in the life of the ordinary believer, turns out to be a *prescriptive* theory which radically revises it. He therefore, again, contradicts his claim that he respects the everyday use of religious language. As we shall see in due course, this is a very damaging criticism for those who want pluralist thinking to provide the theological vision for education.

Joseph Runzo: Absolute Commitment and Religious Relativism

Joseph Runzo[8] has sought to overcome this distortion of traditional belief by developing a Christian relativism that 'would sustain Christian commitment and support Christian claims to truth, without claiming to be the only truth' (1988, page 361). His work is important for education because it is a detailed attempt to provide a rationale for the idea that religious believers can hold their own beliefs with absolute commitment, while, at the same time, recognizing the relative nature of these beliefs. Runzo's purpose is to provide the committed person with a reason for respecting the commitment of others.

One critical problem for any theory of relativism has always been that it is crippled by its own claims. This means that the relativist's assertion that all truth is specific to particular cultures, which appears to be a universal claim, must, if it is true, itself be specific to the culture of the person claiming it and not, therefore, universally true. A real own goal!

In order to overcome this difficulty, Runzo makes a distinction between general theories about truth, and the contents of particular belief systems. General theories like relativism cannot be relative without the possibility of rational discourse being undermined, whereas particular belief systems, such as Christianity, are always relative. Allowing this distinction means that it is possible to talk about relativism being universally true without contradiction. To the non-relativist this distinction seems a somewhat arbitrary assertion.

Runzo begins with two 'facts' that he believes have to be accommodated by any adequate theory of religious belief.

1. The fact that there are a number of mutually exclusive religions. Which one a person belongs to is, for most people, an accident of birth. The differences between these systems are not ultimately resolvable on the standards of public reasoning. In these circumstances, the relativist hypothesis, therefore, seems the most plausible.
2. The fact that believers treat their commitment as absolute, and base this on the belief that their religious propositions are describing reality. To undermine this is to promote scepticism.

Building on these two facts, Runzo's purpose is to show that the acceptance of relativism does not lead to scepticism and is compatible with absolute commitment. He argues that there is 'a fundamental or vital core of beliefs in each religion which is definitive of that very tradition' (1988, page 345), and which, in each case, points to a reality beyond itself. His conclusion is that, in order to accommodate this insight within the relativist thesis, there must be a plurality of different worlds. So, he says that 'the world one lives in—what we call the actual world—is often not the same as the world others live in' (page 59).

There is, according to Runzo, every reason for believers to treat the world they inhabit as real. Runzo, therefore, accommodates the crucial point that believers actually think they are making true statements about the real world. Furthermore, these statements are the basis for the absolute commitments they hold. Lose this and their sense of the reality of God is undermined. As we have seen, it is exactly this point that Hick lost sight of in his denial that doctrines can conflict.

For Runzo, therefore, it is inbuilt in the notion of rationality that there will be a number of true religions. To accept any one of these is rational. He sees nothing irrational in having an absolute commitment to the beliefs of the community in which we have been raised, while, at the same time, accepting the possibility of other people having an absolute commitment to a different set of truths. All believers from different religions have to do is accept that they are living in different worlds. As he puts it, 'for the person of mature monotheistic faith, there will be respected alternative faiths, but there can be no alternative commitment' (page 264). Therefore, absolute commitment and pluralism can exist side by side.

It is important to emphasize that Runzo is not saying that we are at present uncertain about which belief system among the many currently available is the correct one. Rather, he is arguing for 'an ineradicable plurality of mutually incompatible sets of truth' (page 57). Therefore, there are a number of realities or actual worlds (pages 61-2). This is a crucial point, because it is the existence of this plurality of actual worlds that provides believers in the different world religions with the justification for holding their beliefs with absolute commitment.

The big question is whether or not the notion of a number of different real worlds is coherent. Runzo is aware of two potentially fatal criticisms that he seeks to counter.

I : THE PROBLEM OF ISOLATION

His position seems to imply an extreme isolation of people from each other. My Muslim neighbour and I are actually living in two totally different worlds, if Runzo is to be believed, but our experience tells us something very different. We can communicate quite effectively with each other, and find we share many common concerns in our two religions. It simply does not ring true to our experience to say our two worlds are mutually incompatible.

Runzo accepts this point, and explains it by the existence of common ground between people. He sees this as arising from the overlaps that exist between their belief systems. The only other explanation for this ability to communicate is that there is a world of knowledge that is independent of belief systems, and accessible to all people. This position, known as *objectivism*, is clearly untenable for Runzo.

On the basis of this argument Runzo rejects the charge of isolation.

However, to admit this point is actually to undermine his relativist thesis. An analogy may help here. Biological classification rests on the notion of distinct species. Two organisms are said to belong to different species if they cannot reproduce and produce fertile offspring. Sometimes organisms that are geographically isolated from each other may appear to belong to different species. If, however, they are brought into the same environment, and successfully breed, then they can no longer be seen as separate species. The notion of the species would break down altogether if we found that every time we brought together organisms that looked like separate species they in fact ended up breeding.

A parallel argument applies in relation to Runzo's claim there are, like species, a plurality of distinct worlds. If we find that every time these separate worlds come into contact, as they do in modern plural societies, that their members can communicate, reason together, and influence each other, as patently does happen—then this throws considerable doubt on the idea that they are, in fact, different worlds.

What this phenomenon actually leaves us with is the objectivist thesis that the pursuit of knowledge progresses through the construction and testing of hypotheses, which are attempts to describe the reality that exists independently of human thought. However, unlike Hick, the objectivist sees conflicts between belief systems as legitimate, resulting from their different truth claims about reality, which are more or less mistaken. For the objectivist, the task is to remove mistakes from our thinking by debate and study with a view to discovering, as near as is possible, the correct representation of reality. Consideration of a second aspect of Runzo's work confirms that he is, indeed, abandoning his relativism in favour of objectivism in the attempt to ward off his critics.

2: THE NATURE OF ULTIMATE REALITY

A major problem for Runzo is that the idea that there are a number of different real worlds, each with their own truths, in turn makes each of these truths arbitrary. The truth of my world is no more likely to be valid than the truth of someone else's world. However, he believes that there are external criteria for judging the reasonableness of claims to truth. One of these is summed up in the following quote:

> There must be an independent reality which, however indirectly, partially determines the nature of the phenomenal reality which we perceive as real and judge to be true . . . Whether conception and belief actually correspond to reality is, in part, determined by the noumenal, quite independently of our minds. (pages 217–18)

So, for Runzo, there is an independent reality in God, whose thoughts provide the final standard for what can be true and act as a check on the truth of the beliefs we hold (page 225). He argues that the idea that there can be more than one real noumenal God behind the plurality of phenomenal systems is incoherent and unacceptable (Chapter 8). Belief systems, therefore, are not arbitrary, but are answerable to a truth beyond themselves. The closer that our view of reality is to the ultimate noumenal reality, 'the greater the likelihood of success of our purposive activities' (page 246). However, Runzo still wishes to maintain that there is a plurality of phenomenal actual worlds. He accepts that this introduces some uncertainty into our believing, because it opens up the possibility that another belief system might relate to reality more closely than our own. He believes that the *risk* faith takes is that its truth claims do not correctly refer to the noumenal reality; the commitment of faith includes the *trust* that they do (page 258). Such arguments do, however, seem very close to statements like, 'the Creator's knowledge constitutes a conceptual criterion of objectivity' (MacKay, 1987, page 24) and 'disputes should be settled by reference to data independent of anyone's say so' (Helm, 1987, page 37), both of which are taken from a book called *Objective Knowledge*, which, interestingly, is written by a group of Evangelical Christians espousing an objectivist view of religious truth.

So, in the final analysis, Runzo has abandoned his relativist roots because he cannot live with the logic of his main premiss, that there is a plurality of socially constructed realities. In the end, he is arguing the objectivist thesis, which is that there are a number of overlapping interpretations of the one reality, the adequacy of which can be decided by testing their claims against the nature of this reality. He is driven to this position by his, in my opinion commendable, wish to respect the fact that the believer's intention in using religious language is to make statements about reality.

Relativism as a Basis for Tolerance?

It may seem that we have wandered far from the classroom in the exploration of these issues, so now is the time to earth this discussion and explore its implications for education.

We have already seen that the relativist hypothesis is driven by the concern to find a basis for religious tolerance and respect for others, which, it is felt, is not available in absolutist views. Acceptance of relativism is supposed to generate a humility that is conducive to a ready acceptance of those with whom we disagree.

However, what Runzo does not allow for is that such humility is dependent on the objectivist element of his thesis—namely that we are all seeking to describe reality in more and more adequate ways—and not the relativist thesis that there is a plurality of realities. According to his relativist view, there is no reason why I should bother to take account of what can only be the largely incomprehensible beliefs of strange people who occupy a different world from my own. Even if I do manage to come to understand another person's beliefs, that does not mean that I will not find them unacceptable or even repugnant. It is unclear why I should tolerate them, unless there is the possibility that such action will take me further in my own search for truth. The outcome of Runzo's relativist thesis, in fact, is a power struggle between mutually exclusive views of reality. In order to counter the imperialism and intolerance that results from this need to protect one's view of reality against other arbitrary contenders, he has to introduce the objectivist notion that humanity is engaged in the common task of seeking to describe ever more adequately the one noumenal reality. It is, then, possible that someone else's view might be more adequate than my own, so it is important that I treat them with respect and listen carefully to their views.

John Hick's solution also entails that there are a number of different interpretations of the one noumenal reality. Unlike Runzo, however, he is not prepared to accept that their respective doctrines can conflict, because of his concern to find a basis for harmony between the world's religions. However, in coming to this position, he is, in fact, distorting the reality-describing nature of religious belief as it is understood by most believers—something he initially claims *not* to be doing. On Hick's scheme, in order to be tolerant, Christians have to radically revise their theology in a way that makes it quite unrecognizable for many.

Therefore, it seems that both these forms of relativism ultimately fail to provide a coherent basis for tolerance: the one (Runzo) because it denies its own relativism in the concern to respect the reality-claiming nature of religious language that forms the basis for religious commitment; the other (Hick) because, although remaining consistent to its relativism, it denies the reality-claiming nature of religious language, which initially was accepted as fundamental to the religious way of life. Neither, therefore, deals adequately with the reality of religious belief, while, at the same time, remaining consistent to its own relativist hypothesis.

They also both fail to deal adequately with the issue of conflicts of doctrine. Runzo's view accepts that doctrines do describe reality, but avoids the conflict by postulating many different realities. In effect, none of the religions are talking about the same thing, therefore, they cannot conflict. Religious pluralism, therefore, divides humankind into tribes that cannot comprehend each other. Hick, on the other hand, allows for one humanity by seeing religious pluralism as the result of many different descriptions of the same 'Real an sich'. However, he denies the conflict of doctrines that must follow from this by suggesting that they are not to be trusted as accurate description. However, this pulls the carpet out from under commitment, which is an essential of the religious way of life. So, it appears that relativism is somewhat of a lame duck when it comes to providing the basis for respect and tolerance between religions.

Educational Implications

Both these views of relativism have, however, been influential in religious education, largely because the alternative of some form of absolutism has been seen to be abhorrent. Runzo's position underlines the so-called phenomenological method,[9] which emphasizes the importance of encouraging children to stand in other people's shoes. The goal is to teach children to enter into a number of very different religious worlds on the terms laid down by each belief system. The ultimate sophistication is, then, to be able to bracket out our own beliefs in order to appreciate another point of view. This notion is one important part of the rationale of a relatively new, but influential, approach to religious education. This develops a series of structured exercises designed to give pupils the necessary skills to enable them to view the world from another person's perspective.[10]

This view of pluralism makes a nonsense of the idea of a rationality common to all people that can underpin education for all, so it has to be tempered by arguing for the possibility of translation and other means of communication between belief systems. However, doing this sets in motion the drift towards objectivism we noted with Runzo, and the notion of hermetically sealed belief systems begins to break down. Furthermore, it gives no basis for evaluating the worth of different religions, and makes choice a totally arbitrary affair. The believer is a Christian, or Buddhist, or whatever, simply because they are a product of a particular social construction. However, very few religious educationists are prepared to accept that any religion will do. Therefore, they introduce criteria for judging the worth of a religion,[11] but how these criteria are derived without arbitrarily asserting, either that one set of beliefs will provide the norms for judgement, or that there are criteria of truth that exist independently of any belief system, is never made plain.[12]

It is not surprising, therefore, that, among proponents of relativism in education, there is a widespread tendency to adopt the Hickian view that there is one Reality that is experienced through a number of lenses (such as Leech, 1989). This position emphasizes our common humanity. I noted earlier the influence of this approach to pluralism in the recurrent use of the elephant parable (see page 34). The use of optical illusions, showing how one picture can be viewed in two or more different ways, is

47

making the same point (for example, Hammond, *et al.*, 1990, pages 13–14).

However, adopting this view immediately raises the possibility of truth claims conflicting, and, in particular, the absolutist claim that one belief system is superior. This is the *bête noire* of the religious educationist, because of the concern to promote tolerance in society. The response to this is to play down the truth-claiming nature of religious language and to treat it as mysterious, even mythical. In the extreme, religious beliefs are treated as 'simply the vehicles we use to articulate experience' (Hammond, *et al.*, 1990, page 125). Then the emphasis is not on *what* people believe, but on the beneficial *effects* believing has on their lives. A quotation from the *Myth of Christian Uniqueness* (1987), which John Hick coedited with Paul Knitter, illustrates this idea:

> On the basis of their own experience of pondering over the scriptures, the faithful can readily grasp that the power and purpose of biblical language is first of all to call forth a way of life rather than a body of belief. More precisely the Christological language and titles of the New Testament had as their primary purpose not to offer definitive ontological statements about the person or work of Jesus, but to enable men and women to feel the power and attraction of Jesus' vision and then 'to go and do likewise'. (Knitter, 1987, page 196)

The belief that religions describe reality is the casualty of this approach, and commitment, too, is undermined.[13]

Finally, most of the religious educationists who argue for a relativist thesis are unhappy with one of its logical consequences for another reason. If relativism is true, then there should be nothing wrong with our being nurtured in the beliefs of our family as long as they are not treated as absolute, and we tolerate and respect the beliefs of others. Free, individual choice of belief must, after all, be an illusion. However, our analysis of nurture in Chapter 2 suggests that many are concerned that children should transcend the limitations of their family background. For example, in one important article in favour of relativism, we find the author arguing, not for respecting a child's cultural and religious origins, but for each being 'exposed to many modes of thought from the various cultures', so that each 'can choose or synthesise from this' (Phillips-Bell, 1981, page 102). In the final analysis, it appears that absorbing our beliefs from our social environment is not to be welcomed. Individual choice is, in reality, the ideal of many relativists. I have already noted that the core of liberalism is individualism (see page 17). Despite their claims otherwise, these authors are not arguing as *relativists*, but as *liberals*, who place an absolute value on the right of individual choice in matters of religion.

One consequence of promoting liberal individualism from a relativist position is that it entails treating religious language as subjective. In this, religious language is not propositional truth about God, but descriptions of human experience. Choices between different religious belief systems can then easily become little more than opting for that which is most satisfying to a particular person. It is not surprising, therefore, that some religious educationists argue that the role of education is to help each individual choose an authentic language of their own to express those deep therapeutic experiences that are fundamental to true humanity. So, 'prayer . . . is about knowing and being yourself' (Hammond, *et al.*, 1990, page 215).

The problem with this, as I have stressed before, is that most believers do not see their religion this way. To assume such a position as the foundation for common schools will, therefore, not provide an adequate basis for diversity within unity. The only other basis for a concern that children should have the freedom to think and choose for themselves in the matter of religion, is the objectivist position, that there is one reality accessible to all human beings and our beliefs describe this more or less adequately. The aim of learning and debate in religion is, then, that each individual achieves an ever more accurate description of the 'Real an sich'. In other words, it is based on a concern for truth. This is an argument that I shall develop in due course.

CHAPTER FOUR

Relating Theology and Education —an Influential Approach

Introduction

MY ARGUMENT SO far has been that those who see education as an antidote to learning sickness have relied heavily on a particular view of what it means to be rational in relation to religious belief. Sharp distinctions are made by them between the public, rational, and authoritative nature of knowledge, and the private, and controversial nature of religious belief. As a consequence of this, scepticism, individualism, relativism, and subjectivism are seen to characterize the approach to belief that will enable young people to be effective learners in the religious domain. These characteristics are also believed to be those that will encourage respect for, and tolerance of, those with a different faith.

There is no doubt that liberal educationalists are drawing on a respectable tradition of Christian theology in their assertions, but the major problem is that their view of what it means to be rational is not shared by more traditional Christians. It is one view among the many that are available within Christian theology. However, the anti-religionists appear to feel that it is justifiable for teachers to seek, as John Hull puts it, to 'deconstruct' a traditional theological structure so as to 'reveal its religionist features and overcome them by the genuinely religious features of the spiritual tradition' (1992, page 71). Although used in relation to adult education in the Church, Hull also seems to want to apply the idea to schools. So, in the same paragraph, he writes 'the degree to which it is anti-religionist should become one of the criteria for the evaluation of a good new agreed syllabus'. This is a reference to the syllabuses that control the teaching of religious education in common schools in England and Wales. We have to ask how it is that liberal educationalists have come to hold such an evangelical position?

How do they justify seeking to impose a particular view of theology on the population in general? The answer is to be found in the writings of Paul Hirst.

The Influence of Paul Hirst[1]

Probably the most important essay ever published on this theme was Hirst's 'Christian Education: a contradiction in terms?' (1972). In this, he challenged the idea that educational principles can be derived from Christian theology. His assertion was that 'there has emerged in our society a concept of education which makes the whole idea of Christian education a kind of nonsense' (page 77). As mathematics, engineering and farming are governed by principles independent of Christian belief, so, too, is education.

Pivotal to his analysis is the idea of secularization. Hirst sees this as being characterized by 'a decay in the use of religious concepts and beliefs' (page 1). Identifying secularization as a defining feature of life in the modern world leads Hirst to argue that there are two logically distinct concepts of education. The first, 'primitive' notion (primitive because it expresses the view of a primitive tribe) consists of passing on the customs and values of one generation to the next. This view could describe Christian, Humanist, or Buddhist education. The second, 'sophisticated' view is totally different in that it is governed by the autonomous domain of secular knowledge, which is independent of religious concepts. He sees this approach to education as objective, concerned with the development of rationality. The key point is that sophisticated education, like the knowledge it passes on, is based on objective principles that are logically more fundamental than those of a particular religious belief, be it Christian, Buddhist, or Humanist. Its concern is with reason, not controversial belief. It is this secular, 'sophisticated' concept that renders the notion of Christian education a nonsense.

In a later article (1985), he distinguishes four forms of education, the first of which is the same as primitive education as he earlier defined it, and the fourth equates with his earlier sophisticated model. However, he still maintains that model four is the only 'coherent form of education' (page 12). The other three are incoherent. Any coherent approach to education must be independent of theology. To use theological language and criteria in educational discourse is, to put it simply, a mistake.

The use of the term 'primitive' obviously indicates a negative evaluation of forms of education that do aim to pass on beliefs, for example, Christian nurture. By emphasizing the superiority of the 'sophisticated' public domain, with its concern for objective, secular knowledge, Hirst is implicitly denigrating the value of the 'primitive', private domain.

This Hirstian view is well-illustrated by a more recent article by John Wilson. In it he says:

> The aims of anything that can respectably be called religious *education* . . . are common ground to any rational person . . . to talk about Jewish or Protestant education in religion must be seen to be as silly as talking about Jewish or Protestant education in science or literature . . . this does not mean it is wrong for groups or individuals to be committed . . . it is only when they attempt to pass on their particular and partisan commitments to children that danger ensues. For children are not the property of their parents or any group which has a partisan commitment . . . they are potentially rational and autonomous adults. (1992, pages 22–3)

The continuing influence of Hirst's views can also be discerned in the work of Michael Grimmitt. In a brief, but highly significant, postscript to his book *Religious Education and Human Development* (1987a), he argues that he has been utilizing a non-theological rationale for education. By this he means that religious educators are essentially 'secular educators concerned with the educational value of studying religion and religions' (page 258). The prime commitment of the teacher is, therefore, 'to the achievement of educational goals by way of a process that conforms to general educational principles' (page 258). Here, Grimmitt is asserting the autonomy of educational principles against attempts to domesticate them by the religions. The rationale for including religion in education is that it contributes to independent, educational goals, and not for its own theological purposes (1991). Theology cannot preach to education.

Grimmitt's justification for holding to this Hirstian notion of the autonomy of education seems to be that its goal of humanization is objective in a sense that religious goals are not. Humanization is one of the givens of human existence (1987a, pages 69–92) and, therefore, is universally applicable (that is, secular) in a way that religious norms are not. The reason for including the study of religion in the curriculum must be to promote this educational objective.

Hirst's influence is, perhaps, most starkly illustrated in Grimmitt's comment that a specifically religious view of education would entail developing Christian geography, Christian social studies, and so on. As far as Grimmitt is concerned, this is 'clearly a nonsense' (1987a, page 260). However, he gives no supporting argument for this bold assertion, seeming to regard it as self-evident, although he does concede that it is a position held by some Muslims. A conclusion like this can only be reached by drawing heavily on Hirstian arguments, which seek to establish the autonomy of the disciplines from religion. However, earlier in the book, Grimmitt explicitly rejects Hirst's position in favour of the relativist view that knowledge is a product of social experience (1987a, pages 18–31). It is hard to see why Christian geography is clearly a nonsense if knowledge is, as he states, 'a social construct, socially related and socially relative' (page 23).

The Contribution of John Hull[2]

Grimmitt's brief discussion draws on a more extensive discussion of this topic by John Hull. Hull accepts the autonomy of education, but his main criticism of Hirst is that this does not mean that theology cannot make valid comments on education (page 198). He makes two main points to support this. First, he argues that Hirst, in refusing to allow it any role, has failed to make a fundamentally important distinction between two possible functions for theology: an *illuminating* one in which theology supports educational principles arrived at independently of theological ideas, and an *adjudicating* one in which educational issues are determined by theological ideas (page 239). An example of illumination would be to use Jesus' teaching methods to illustrate the educational rejection of indoctrination. An example of adjudication would be to derive all educational principles from the phrase 'the fear of the Lord is the beginning of wisdom and knowledge of the Holy One is understanding' (Proverbs 9:10). Hull regards illumination as legitimate, but not adjudication, as this would violate the autonomy of education. Second, he argues that Hirst lumps all theology together in a naive way. While recognizing that some forms of Christian theology can only lead to a primitive conception of education, he argues that there are others 'in which critical enquiry and controversial examination flow directly and necessarily from the values and beliefs to which the theology is committed' (page 241).

Hull develops his position by first defining the task of theology as rational thinking about the religious consciousness in order to 'articulate, to clarify and to conceptualize' it (page 253). As there are a number of different religious consciousnesses, it follows that there will be a number of different theologies, of which only some will be able to dialogue with education in a way that respects its autonomous, secular status. Furthermore, the nature of theology is such that, although anyone can study it, a person can only do theology on the subject matter of their own beliefs. It follows, therefore, that, as not everyone is religiously committed, theology of education as a 'doing' activity is limited to those individuals who have religious beliefs to articulate. It is essentially a minority activity.

Hull contrasts this with the position in relation to the philosophy of education. Unlike theology, which is related to specific commitments, such as Judaism or Islam, philosophy is secular 'in that it is concerned with nothing but good thinking of a philosophic kind' (page 258). Therefore, it is a universal activity characteristic of 'the community of all rational people' (page 259). The conclusion is that 'you can thus do philosophy only if you are rational, but you can do theology only if you are religious' (page 259). We can choose whether or not to be religious, but we cannot choose whether or not to be rational, as this is a constituent of being human. It follows, therefore, that *theology* of education is optional, whereas *philosophy* of education is not. Philosophy is a secular activity; theology is not.

This distinction has very important implications for the relationship between theology and education. The critical factor is the status of education. Hull assumes that it is the same as philosophy—an activity rooted in rationality, common to all people and, therefore, more basic than optional ways of life, such as the religious (page 260). He expresses this by saying that education is a 'secular' subject, an area from which the sacred has been removed, but that is shared by all people because of their common rationality. Thus, it is to be equated with objectivity. Theology must respect this; it is not in a position to tell education it should be something else as education, being secular, is logically prior.

Theology, therefore, can only provide illuminating insights on educational principles; it cannot seek to adjudicate on them. 'It remains a carefully limited enterprise, which must not, in criticizing education, lose respect for the secularity of education' (page 263). Theology is the servant not the queen, and, in its relationship with education, must take its chance alongside other optional disciplines, *earning* the right to comment (1985b, page 42). There is, according to Hull, no shame in this for 'it is better to be a dog harnessed with other dogs helping to pull a real cart . . . than to be a solitary performing dog having nothing serious to do in the outside world' (1985b, page 44).

One very important outcome of this influential analysis comes when asking how individual teachers are to view their own religious commitments when working as educators. Hirst's early view is clear (1972). Personal belief is a private matter, having nothing to do with teachers' public responsibilities, where they are answerable to the authority of rational principles alone. Drawing on Hirst's views, other religious educators have written that 'if a teacher becomes conscious that his religious beliefs are conflicting with his educational obligations, the latter should determine what he does in the classroom' (Cox, 1983, page 57), and 'the RE teacher must subordinate his personal to his professional commitment' (Johns, 1981). Grimmitt adopts a similar position in arguing that a teacher's prime commitment must be to educational goals as their first priority (1981, pages 50–1, 1987a, pages 258–9, 1991, page 78).

Hull, too, is concerned that teachers preserve the distinction between their public, professional responsibilities, and their personal faith. However, he wants to 'avoid relegating the personal religious faith of the teacher to the private sphere' (1980a, page 1) because he sees the danger of religious education being taught by passionless teachers with empty hearts. Therefore, he urges teachers to find a theology that will enable them to be committed to an educational approach, without compromising their personal religious commitment. However, he believes that only certain theologies can produce such an adequate theology of education.

We can now see how it is that Hull feels justified in insisting on an anti-religionist theology as the basis for education. It is, to put it simply, the one that accords most closely with educational principles. As educational principles are rational, public, and objective, this happy concurrence presumably gives anti-religionist theologies an authority that is not enjoyed by other theologies. The conclusion, therefore, is straightforward. The authority enjoyed by education is enough to provide the justification necessary for making anti-religionist theology normative in schools. Anti-religionist theology is justified on grounds of reason alone.

A CRITIQUE OF THE HULL THESIS

Hull recognizes that his analysis is open to two potential criticisms (pages 260–1). First, he realizes that it will not stand up if the assertion that education is independent of theology is successfully challenged. Second, he accepts that, if being religious is a defining attribute of being human, then theology takes on a similar status to philosophy. Hull argues that anyone making these two criticisms will not succeed as they are not facing up to the process of secularization. In other words, they are not accepting the fact that theology is a minority activity and so cannot control a public activity like education. I will now try to show that these two criticisms are, in fact, successful. I will deal with this in some detail, because it is such an important point, for, if Hull is correct, there can be no distinctive Christian vision for education; only a secular vision with a Christian gloss.

1: The Independent Rationality of Education

Hull's case for the independence of education rests on one critical distinction between the universal, secular activity of philosophy based on reason alone, and the optional activity of theology based on particular, controversial beliefs. The conclusion he draws from this distinction appears to be that it is legitimate to require all humans to think philosophically, but one cannot require this of them in relation to theology. Philosophy is a public activity; theology a private one. Philosophy, and, by implication, education, has a universal, uncontroversial authority that theology does not.

The first difficulty with this to consider regards his use of the word 'philosophy'. Hull seems to understand it simply as the process of thinking in a rational fashion. To practise philosophy, then, would involve thinking consistently, coherently, without contradiction, and with due regard to relevant evidence. Therefore, it is independent of culture and belief. On this basis, practising philosophy and being rational are equated. It is not possible, then, to stop thinking philosophically, because this would be to step outside rationality.

However, the fact that philosophy, in the sense of good thinking, is universal actually trivializes the point that Hull is making. This is because it ignores the role that value judgements and presuppositions play in philosophy. To say that I must think consistently or give regard to evidence is simply to provide me with a tool or skill that I can use to any purpose or end,[3] and this tool is as essential for the theologian as for the philosopher. In this sense, we can probably distinguish a universal activity called rationality—or philosophy as Hull prefers to call it. The crucial questions, however, are what are the presuppositions I build on, and what are the ends I regard as valuable in the process of thinking?

To use the term philosophy in the way Hull does masks the fact that there are many different philosophies—existentialist, Marxist, Buddhist, and so on—all of which exhibit the universal characteristics of rationality (to different degrees). The characters of each of these are determined by their presuppositions. It is as ridiculous to argue that something called philosophy exists independently of particular belief systems as it is to say that meat can be found independently of its particular manifestations as chicken, pork, lamb, and so on.

Hull is aware of this problem and notes that 'naturally philosophy of education cannot avoid working from within a particular tradition' (page 258). None of these are universal, in the sense that Hull argues rationality is. This appears to put philosophy in a similar position to theology. However, he seems to ignore this in the rest of what he says. It certainly seems correct that rationality is *not* optional, but the particular *form* of philosophy or theology that we adopt when using it most certainly is. In both cases, commitment to particular presuppositions is involved.

The points I have made about philosophy as a value-laden activity also apply to education. If education is 'a process by, in and through which pupils may begin to explore what it is and what it means to be human' (Grimmitt, 1982, page 141), then we are dealing with an area where presuppositions are very important. Theology has a central concern with the question of what it means to be human and there is no logical reason for its concerns being excluded from debates about the aims of education.[4] So, for example, the Islamic emphasis on the importance of submitting one's life to the will of Allah would lead to the implementation of a very different teaching process to that of one where the liberal goal of freedom of choice was paramount.

Furthermore, even if religious education *were* promoting a supposedly non-religious, secular goal like humanization, it is very difficult to see how theological criteria can be excluded from any assessment of the most appropriate material to select from Christianity, or any other religion, to promote this goal (Astley, 1988). The fact that Hull wishes to exclude miracle stories from the religious education of young children on the grounds that they are 'incomprehensible and alienating stories of other worldly wonders' (1991d, page 46), would seem to have quite a lot to do with applying theological criteria.

Like Grimmitt, Hull's position is heavily dependent on Hirst's thesis of the autonomy of education. However, this leaves both Hull and Grimmitt with a basic contradiction in their thinking. Establishing the independent rationality of education depends on the notion that objective, rational knowledge exists. In other words, it means that knowledge, and, hence, education, is independent of culture and ideology. However, Grimmitt's work is based on the rejection of this view. Indeed, on the page before that on which he asserts the independent rationality of education, he states 'there is no possibility of a rationale for religious education which is ideology and value free' (1987a, page 257). That the same is true for Hull can be seen from his assertion that 'ideological thinking is inescapable. It is a quality of human action and commitment to think in ideological terms' (1985a, page 53). He also notes that 'reading Paulo Freire has alerted many religious educators to the social, political and religious values hidden behind an apparently neutral and pro-fessional education' (1985b, page 48).

Therefore, this question must be asked, how can a process that is contextually dependent and subject to ideological influence (Grimmitt, 1987a, pages 35–9) have an independent, universally applicable rationality? One answer Grimmitt gives is to point to the value-free process of humanization that education promotes. This, though, suffers from the same defect as Hull's position on philosophy; it does not get us anywhere. This is because, as Grimmitt himself points out (1987b, page 165), a value like humanization can only be applied by being interpreted from within a particular belief system. It depends for its application on presuppositions about what it means to be human. If education is, by its nature, contextual, and, although not an ideology itself, subject to ideological influence (1987a, page 35), it follows that it cannot have an independent ration-ality. Different ideologies have very different views on what it means to be human. In continuing to argue for the independence thesis, Grimmitt and Hull are both behaving like the butcher who claims his shop only stocks pure meat independent of any particular animal species.

Grimmitt does concede this criticism at one point, and argues that the perspective adopted by education should be one 'which is consistent with the dominant ideological assumptions of the majority of our pupils' (1987a, page 46). In the modern world, he argues, this is secular. However, the logic of this argument is that there is no inherent reason why, in a uniformly religious society, that majority perspective should not be theological. He himself agrees that religions function as ideologies (Grimmitt, 1987a, pages 46–50). However, Grimmitt would want to call this nurture, not education, as, for him, education has a rationality independent of religion. So, the consequence of Grimmitt's arguments appears to be that *education* is a process dominated by a majority secular perspective, while *nurture* is dominated by a majority religious perspective. Both, however, are ideologi-cally determined; neither has an independent rationality. Thus, no justifiable distinction can be made between them such that one is deemed particular and private, and the other public with universal authority—rather they simply reflect the religious make-up of different societies.

Therefore, it appears that the case for the independent

rationality of education just does not stand up. However, both Grimmitt and Hull have one chief reason for feeling that it is important that it should.

In the plural context, they both regard it as quite unacceptable for education to impose one theological view on everyone (for example, Grimmitt, 1987a, page 39). With this I agree. However, their assumption is that, if education is not theologically independent, the only alternative is for it to impose the beliefs of one religion, but then education for all, or diversity within unity, becomes impossible. Because there seems to be no middle way, both Grimmitt and Hull support the independence of education, using arguments based on the universal applicability of reason. In Chapter 7, I will suggest that this polarization is not necessary and that a middle way is possible.

2: Religion as Constitutive of Humanity—Homo Religiosus

As we have seen, Hull's concern regarding the first criticism of his thesis is that it domesticates education by making it subject to theology. His concern about the second criticism is that it universalizes religion (page 261). It involves the assertion that being religious, like being rational, is an inescapable part of being human. If this is true, one cannot, for example, think about a discipline like education without thinking theologically. It must have an adjudicating role. Hull dubs this the 'homo religiosus argument' (page 261), and rejects it. Empirical observation alone shows that it is quite possible to be human without being religious.

What, then, is the basis of the 'homo religiosus' strategy?[5] The fundamental core lies in its definition of religion. The argument is that all humans seek to make some sense of their existence. Seeking to make sense of our existence is a religious activity. As we all do this, we are, therefore, all religious.

The objection to this is that it entails the fallacy of counting atheism, Marxism, or secular humanism as religions, on the grounds that they are belief systems that help some people make sense of their existence. To this, proponents of 'homo religiosus' reply that this is legitimate because these beliefs function in the same way for their adherents as theistic beliefs do for theirs.[6]

However, the argument has not established as much as is claimed. The view that atheism functions in the life of the atheist in the same way that theism functions in the life of a theist has only demonstrated that atheism is an *alternative* to theism. This does not make atheism and theism *the same thing*. An example will illustrate this point. Wealth and poverty are two possible ways of living life, which function in the same way in the life of the individual. For example, whether we are wealthy or poverty stricken will be an important influence on decisions we make about our style of housing. However, it is clearly a nonsense to then say that they are examples of the same thing; rather they are alternative states of existence. In the same way, it is a nonsense to insist that humanists are religious simply because they have ultimate concerns that affect their decisions in the same manner that a religious person's beliefs affect theirs.

In the end, the argument only establishes that people are 'homo ultimus concernus', not 'homo religiosus'. There are alternative ways of interpreting ultimate concerns, some of which are religious, and some of which are non-religious. Therefore, the conclusion is that religious and non-religious ways of life are alternatives and, hence, both optional. The religious option has certain features, such as the worship of God, which are not present in the non-religious option. As a result, I seem to be in agreement with John Hull in rejecting the 'homo religiosus' strategy.

However, it is possible to develop a different strategy to the 'homo religiosus' argument that *does* succeed in establishing the legitimacy of theology having an adjudicating, rather than simply an illuminating, function in education. This anticipates some of the arguments as to an alternative theory of religious knowledge that will be outlined in Chapter 6.

A suitable starting point is to assume that there are certain facts of human existence. Two examples would be that we all hold to beliefs and values in order to make sense of our lives, and that we all have to accept the basic rules of rational thought. I have already argued that these insights are, of themselves, trivial. This is because, in order to be able to utilize such facts, for example in education, and avoid the 'so what' rejoinder, they have to be set within an interpretative framework. The presuppositions and values of this will give these facts direction and significance. So, for example, as an Evangelical Christian, the fact that everyone has beliefs and values means that I engage in evangelism because I believe that some of these beliefs are both wrong and destructive and have eternal consequences. Existentialists, however, might treat all beliefs as equally legitimate. For them what matters is the authenticity of the individual freely choosing these beliefs, not their particular content. It should be immediately obvious that these two very different 'ultimate concerns' will produce two very different approaches to education. The same applies to atheistic concerns, Islamic concerns, humanist concerns, and so on—the list is endless. Education cannot, then, have some secular rationality independent of the belief frameworks of 'homo ultimus concernus'. In each case, these beliefs will have an adjudicating role, determining what the educational goals are to be, and will not simply be providing some gloss or illumination on an independent discipline, the aims of which are determined on the basis of rational principles alone.

This means that a theist will give a theological interpretation of educational values based on religious beliefs. A humanist will, no doubt, offer a secular view based on secular beliefs. Reasonable people will, therefore, differ on which is correct. Although this argument has not established the truth of 'homo religiosus', it does establish the *equal* legitimacy of approaching education from either a secular *or* a religious perspective. There is no independent rationality for education; the secular and religious views are both live options. There can be no justification, then, for demanding that the religious person works with a secular view of education on the basis that the secular view represents public, universal values and the religious view private, particular ones. Thus, with Hull, I accept that the religious view is optional, but, contra to Hull, I also accept that the same applies to the secular view.

A further, simple point follows from these arguments when they are applied to religious education. An atheist, wishing to engage in religious education, has to *do* theology by making some judgement on the significance of religious language, and what it means to hold a religious belief in a rational way. (Of course, the atheist's use of theological language will not presuppose faith in God.) Therefore, a rationale for *religious education* cannot avoid being theological. In this restricted sense, everyone engaged in religious education is religious. There cannot be any universal, secular rationale for the subject, if by secular it is meant that an error has been committed by introducing theological language and criteria. There can, however, be a secular rationale if by this is meant that one of the secular theologies popular in some quarters is utilized as the underpinning of the subject. However, such a rationale is still theological.

Some Final Comments

In this chapter, I have argued against the notion that education has an independent rationality. Instead, I have suggested that it is always ideologically determined. I have accepted the point that a religious view of education is optional, but countered this by showing that the same applies to the so-called secular view. Therefore, I have challenged the argument that the secular view has an objectivity and authority not enjoyed by a religious view. Which of these two we find satisfactory will, in the end, depend on the particular presuppositions we personally hold. Reasonable people will differ on this. Finally, I have argued that religious education is an exception because, in order to discuss aims, one has to use theological criteria. This means that there has to be a theological rationale. In this narrow sense, every religious educator is 'homo religiosus'.

CHAPTER FIVE

Dilemmas for Secular Education

IT MAY BE helpful at this stage to take stock of the implications of my argument so far. Perhaps I can begin with a publicity leaflet produced by the Professional Council for Religious Education (PCfRE), the largest association of religious education teachers in the UK. In that it is stated that the 'PCfRE is a purely professional body, independent of any particular faith'. This presumably distinguishes it from my employing organization, the Association of Christian Teachers, which, I assume, is not *'purely* professional' because it caters for the needs of a particular faith group. The same would no doubt also apply to the Catholic Teachers Fellowship, the Jewish Educational Bureau, the Muslim Educational Trust and the British Humanist Association Education Committee, to name but a few.

What, then, is the significance of this emphasis on 'pure' professionalism? Traditionally, it has been utilized to distinguish education from so-called confessional activities like nurture, which aim to further the religious goal of promoting faith. This is a helpful distinction in so far as it reminds us that what I have called common schools are not the same as churches. In the latter, a faith commitment can form the framework of all the activities. In the former, it cannot.

However, the difficulties arise when it is assumed that the professional activity is somehow superior to confessional activities because it is public in a sense that they are not. The distinction between professional and confessional then ceases to identify activities appropriate to particular contexts and becomes evaluative instead. To give an example, an article I once wrote was criticized by the then Chairperson of the Association of RE Advisers and Inspectors because it was said to 'be written purely from a faith perspective', and had not, therefore, 'applied that broader professional view'. On behalf of the Association, he requested the opportunity to write a reply article, because he felt that advice to teachers should 'come from those who recognise and understand the curriculum process'.[1] It seems that because I wrote as a Christian, my views were assumed to be of no consequence. They were not, by a priori definition, professional. Likewise, to begin a training day for teachers with Christian prayer, as has happened on courses I have spoken at in Northern Ireland and for English dioceses, would, no doubt, be professionally suspect to some because the independence from a particular faith had not been maintained.

What I am suggesting in this book is that the understanding of professionalism that has developed in religious education over the last thirty years has created a culture which is antagonistic to certain forms of Christian faith. To use Hugh Montefiore's words, it is not 'Gospel friendly'.[2] I am certainly not suggesting that this is overt in the thinking of most teachers, nor that the PCfRE adopts this as a matter of policy. As an enthusiastic member of this organization, I would deny that straight away. What I am saying is that we need to be critically aware of the unexamined baggage that attaches to this notion of pure professionalism.

It is important, therefore, that the idea that a professional approach to education is independent of any particular faith is unpacked very carefully. If not, it can easily degenerate into discrimination against more traditional forms of religious belief. Indeed, in some cases, it even sinks into antagonism towards religion itself. The first four chapters of this book have shown how this can happen. This has created a culture that is antagonistic to those Christians who believe in authoritative revelation, the exclusive claims of Jesus Christ, the propositional nature of doctrines like the Resurrection, the importance of nurture, and an absolute commitment to Christ in daily life. This would include, among others, conservative Roman Catholics, most members of the Black-led churches, the Evangelicals and most members of the Orthodox churches, to name but a few.

To recap on how this has happened, we need to take particular note of a crucial link in the chain of the argument. It is the attempt to find an uncontroversial view of education that is independent of religious belief, by defining it in terms of the promotion of that which is distinctively human. So, Hirst and Hull have both argued that education is concerned with rationality and Grimmitt that it is concerned with humanization. Because, they say, these are givens of the human condition, educational values are public in a way that values derived from particular controversial belief systems are not. Diversity within unity is, it is argued, achieved by making education dependent only on the facts of what it means to be human, and keeping it independent of particular controversial beliefs. Then there is no problem because all religions can accept these facts on which education is based.

The difficulty with this approach is that it ignores one important point. Namely, that general concepts like rationality or humanization cannot exist by themselves. To be applied, they have to be interpreted from within a particular belief system. So, any educational values based on such concepts are always specific to particular traditions. We find, therefore, that there is an important shift in the argument. It hinges on the recognition that not all religions *do* accept these so-called facts *as interpreted* by liberal education theory. The assumption is that they *should*. So, we start by taking the seemingly neutral facts of human experience as providing a basis for unity because they *are* accepted by everyone. We finish by seeing them as providing this basis because they *ought* to be accepted by everyone in their liberal form. The description has become prescription.

The educationist's search, then, is for theologies that concur with, or, as Hull puts it, illuminate, these prescriptive, public educational principles. These theologies are deemed to enjoy the same authoritative status as the educational principles they illuminate. My analysis suggests that this sort of theology displays the following four features.

1. An acceptance of the notion that individual choice of religion is of ultimate value. The transmission of belief through a faith community is, therefore, 'non-', or even 'anti-', educational. There is, then, a strong undercurrent of individualism, which can be attributed to the widespread influence of the philosophy of liberalism.

2. An acceptance of the notion that, because religious beliefs are controversial, they should only be held in a tentative fashion. They should, therefore, always be open to revision. Absolute commitment is regarded as unacceptable as there is never enough evidence for a religious belief to warrant the confidence this exhibits. Rational religious believers are expected to regard the future of their beliefs as open. Doubt, or at least the expectation of falsification of their beliefs, is considered to be a

virtue. This is in contrast to attitudes to the more public forms of knowledge (and, indeed, educational theory itself), which are deemed to have an objective, non-controversial authority.

3. Related to the previous point is the acceptance of the relativity of religious beliefs. They are seen to be products of our social experience. This leads to an emphasis on a pluralist theology of other religions as against absolutist positions, as there seems to be no legitimate reason for anyone regarding their religious 'truth' as any more valid than that of another person.

4. Finally, there is an emphasis on the instrumental function of religious belief. This means that the important thing about a religion is its effects rather than its propositions. This is allied with a tendency to accept a subjectivist account of the nature of religious language, which sees doctrine as describing the inner world of human experience. This is in contrast to a realist view, which sees it as making statements about the nature of an external reality.

Therefore, I find myself in agreement with Edward Hulmes in his conclusion that a particular attitude on what is to count as valid religious knowledge is widespread, perhaps even normative, in the educational system of Britain (see page 13). Some faith communities are describing this as secular humanism. A commentator on primary religious education called it 'secular theology' (Bates, 1992, page 109). In my opinion, it is more accurate to refer to it as 'radical Christian liberalism',[3] as it has its origins in a particular form of Christian theology, *radicalism*, which has been heavily influenced by the liberal ideal of *individualism*.

However, there are affinities between this form of thought and secularism. First, it makes theological reflection irrelevant by privatizing it. So, teachers are told that their faith is irrelevant to their educational responsibilities, or, and perhaps this is even more worrying, they are told to find a theology that resonates with these responsibilities. Theological truth, therefore, is to be judged by secular educational criteria. Second, it can develop into an attack on the religious way of life *per se*. So, we have seen that, for some educationists, there is an inevitable clash between educational aims and those of religious nurture. This clash is particularly acute in the case of those faith communities that adopt a more absolutist view of religious knowledge. However, it has to be admitted that there is a reluctance in the educational literature to pursue the logic of this conclusion. Very few writers are prepared to accept that the role of education is to combat the nurturing activity of faith communities. Rather, they seek to present education and nurture as complementary activities, appropriate to different contexts, and do not face up to the antipathy that is really there. The reason for this reluctance becomes apparent when another important aspect of secular education is examined in more detail.

The Ideals of Secular Education

A characteristic feature of educational debates over the last thirty years has been a growing sensitivity to the implications of the reduced public role that religion, and especially Christianity, plays in modern society. There is also an increased awareness that British society is now comprised of many faiths coexisting together under largely secular norms, but with a residual Christian structure. This situation has developed in a social and political context where democratic values, with their emphasis on freedom and justice, form the framework for public life.

Common schools, therefore, have to accommodate a social order in which people adhere to fundamentally different sets of beliefs, as well as meeting the needs of all pupils. Developing a legitimate response to this social and political context is a major challenge for those seeking to relate religious belief and education. In particular, the question of how the many theological beliefs present in modern society are to interact with this public educational enterprise is of crucial significance.

John Patten, the Secretary of State for Education [at the time of writing], discovered the complexity of this task on 5 March, 1993. On that day, he made a speech outlining plans for national model syllabuses for religious education. Their purpose would be to help children grow up with positive moral and spiritual values. In particular, children needed a 'fuller understanding of the beliefs and values that have bound communities together over many generations in our country'. He announced that he had written to church leaders to seek their advice and assistance.

The speech was greeted with howls of protest. As one Muslim leader put it, 'it seems as though Mr Patten has overlooked the fact that Britain is not just Anglican or Roman Catholic. The minority faiths don't seem to be fully acknowledged in the consultation process'. He welcomed the emphasis on spiritual and moral values, but feared a resurgence of Christian nationalism. Humanists were equally alarmed at the suggestion that moral values had to be underpinned by Christianity. In basking in the consensus that schools should promote spiritual and moral values, Mr Patten had ignored the pluralism of interpretations that exists as to exactly what those values should be.

What Mr Patten had forgotten was that a democratic society has to take account of the aspirations of *all* its citizens. It can only do this by tolerating significant diversity within the context of a unity provided by public values. It should not attempt to build these public values on the religious beliefs of one particular group of citizens. To attempt to do so is, ultimately, self-destructive as it will engender resentment and, possibly, conflict. Public values have to attract a good deal of common support.

One way of describing the approach to religious education that will achieve this is to say that it should be fair (Jackson, 1984; McLaughlin, 1992b). By this is meant that it should respect both the pupils, by not seeking to impose a faith on them, and the religions that are its subject matter, by presenting them as far as is possible from the believer's perspective.[4]

Such ideals are often described as secular, a term that is meant to capture the fact that no one system of 'religious' beliefs should dominate the public life of society. It is important to distinguish this from a 'secularist' approach, which is positively antagonistic to religious belief. The secular society values the contribution of the many different religions within a framework of values designed to promote community harmony. The secularist society seeks to eradicate the influence of religion, except perhaps in the purely private sphere. So, the ideals of Gandhi's India were secular, whereas those of Mao's China were secularist. The secular society is pluralistic, this term being used here in the descriptive sense of containing many religious traditions and not in the normative sense of prescribing a particular theology of religions.[5] Here, each citizen is free to live by the tenets of their own religion, but in the public context is expected to accept and work alongside those of the many different faiths that make up society. In contrast, the secularistic society is monolithic, imposing an atheistic framework of belief on its citizens.

Thus, the public institutions of a secular, as opposed to a secularist, society cannot legitimately seek to propagate one particular religion. Rather, they are restricted to the role of promoting the freedoms associated with their democratic, religiously 'neutral' status. The secular State should not press its citizens to hold, or conform to, particular religious beliefs. Brian Crittenden describes this as 'the pluralist principle of respect for diversity in areas of belief where people may reasonably differ' (1988, page 126). Such ideals are widely accepted in the literature on religious education. Michael Grimmitt provides a good example of someone who supports them. Thus, he argues that education should not set out to promote one particular form of religion, because the authority that gives particular beliefs their absolute status for a faith community is not normative for most of the participants in the educational process (1987a, page 39).

However, secular schools (what I have called common schools earlier) are not neutral in the sense of being value-free zones. This is why I put inverted commas round the word neutral in the previous paragraph. They do embody norms and values. Integral to the view of the secular realm that is being proposed here, is the belief that schools, as State institutions, have a responsibility to promote social harmony. This position is central to Government policy as the following quote shows:

> The Government also attaches great importance to the role of religious education and collective worship in helping to promote among pupils a clear set of personal values and beliefs. They have a role in promoting respect for and understanding of those with different beliefs and religious practices from their own, based on a rigorous study of the different faiths. This country has a long history of religious freedom which should be preserved. (DFE, 1994, page 10)

In a speech to the Association of RE Advisers and Inspectors in 1992, David Pascall, the then Chairman of the National Curriculum Council, said:

> Learning about religions has more than an intellectual and practical application. For the stability of our society, and the maintaining of good personal relationships and behaviour towards others, it is vital that, through the increased under-

standing of our beliefs and practices, our children come to respect the right of others to hold beliefs different from their own and both accept and value the many cultures, religions and traditions evident around them while remaining secure in their own. (paragraph 26)

There is, then, a considerable body of opinion that sees the promotion of social cohesion as a major function of common schools. Most syllabuses of religious education identify this as being of central importance.[6] This certainly means that education should not discriminate against a particular religion, unless, of course, the religion is itself a major threat to social cohesion. However, if the arguments I have advanced are correct, it is fairly clear that such discrimination is inherent in the culture of professionalism that is currently influential in religious education. How has this basic contradiction come about?

The source of this difficulty is actually straightforward. It arises from the attempt to combine two strategies to relating theology and education.

The first strategy is that favoured by Paul Hirst, which identifies education with the promotion of rationality. Therefore, it has an objective and universal status that gives it authority over controversial religious beliefs. According to this view, the rational and the secular are equated. In it is to be found the genesis of such dichotomies as professional/confessional, education/nurture, sophisticated/primitive, philosophy/theology, and public/private; all of which we have found in the literature on this subject.

There are two possible outcomes of this position. The first is that all religions are treated as equally irrational and none of them are allowed a public educational role. This is certainly fair between the religions, but it radically privatizes them in a way that is quite unacceptable (except to rationalists) in a multifaith society. The second is to seek to identify a rational way of being religious that can then be treated as normative in schools. In other words, it is the attempt to unite religions by encouraging them to adopt what might be called a universal theology. This seems more sympathetic to religions by allowing them a public role, but, as I have shown, poses a radical threat to more traditional forms of belief. Furthermore, it makes religious belief subject to the authority of Western liberalism.

The second strategy picks up what Brian Crittenden has called the pluralist principle, with its emphasis on fairness and respect for diversity. This recognizes that there is no way of finally deciding between religions on grounds of rationality alone. People may reasonably differ on this issue. Furthermore, it accepts that educational aims will be influenced by religious beliefs. In this situation, it is not legitimate for State schools to impose one religious viewpoint. The educational task, in Michael Grimmitt's words, is 'not to impose your particular construct of reality on the children you teach' (1987a, page 27). In common schools, it is quite inappropriate that the norms of one religious tradition should be considered prescriptive for everyone (1987a, pages 39–40).

The problem with many works on religious education is that they seek to pursue both of these strategies at the same time. This is simply not possible because they are mutually exclusive. It is inconsistent to espouse the pluralist principle, while, at the same time, seeking to impose radical Christian liberalism. The incredible thing is that this is often done in the name of tolerance. The conscience is salved because it is believed that rationality demands this. However, this ignores the fact that what exactly constitutes rational religious belief is a matter on which people may reasonably differ. It, thereby, opens the gates to those with power to impose their view of rationality on the population at large.

If rationality and fairness are to be held together in common schools, we need to be able to answer two questions. First, is it possible to develop an understanding of religious belief that supports the pluralist principle by being true to the way in which most religious believers hold their faith, but that also distinguishes between rational and irrational ways of believing and discourages tribalistic attitudes? I shall make the attempt in Chapter 6. Second, is it possible to develop an understanding of the relationship between theology and education that does not entail adopting one view of religion as normative, but, rather, provides a basis for participation by all religious communities in the plural society? This question will be the subject of Chapter 7. Finding answers to these two questions is essential if a system of education for all, which really provides a basis for diversity within unity, is to be developed, and if the sorts of contradictions I identified earlier are to be avoided.

—

PART II

Transforming the Foundations of Religious Education

CHAPTER SIX

Towards an Alternative View
of Rational Religion

Introduction

THE FIRST PART of this book has been a sustained criticism of influential liberal views of education, so I wish to begin this second part by making it quite clear that there is much in the liberal view that I see as right and helpful. I do accept that there is a problem with religious learning sickness in our society. I agree with the liberal educator's diagnosis of the symptoms—intolerance, fear of change, unwillingness to learn, tribal attitudes, and so forth. Indeed, I am very concerned about their effects. I also believe that education has a role to play in combatting these. My argument has been with a particular liberal analysis of the cause of this sickness and with its prescription for the cure.

The purpose of this second part of the book is not, then, to replace the liberal view with something totally different, but, rather, to attempt to redefine it. Central to the success of this project will be to establish a viable distinction between rational and irrational forms of religious belief. If we cannot do that, religion is left as something arbitrary. At the same time, my analysis must respect the reality of religious belief as it is lived out and experienced by people throughout the world. I will have failed if my diagnosis of 'healthy' belief undermines traditional religion. This is exactly the problem with the liberal view I have criticized. Absolute commitment and the communal nature of traditional religious belief have to be accommodated. At the same time, the importance of openness to new learning, and of respect for those who have beliefs different to our own have to be affirmed. These are central to a responsible approach to education.[1]

The Rationality of Commitment

Perhaps the most important question to be faced is how can it ever be rational to be committed to religious beliefs to the degree that we base our whole lives on them, perhaps even die for them? For many liberals such an idea is repugnant.

Absolute commitment implies a stubborn holding on to a fixed body of beliefs and an inability to learn. This is fundamentalism, and it frightens liberals. Therefore, they seek to divorce their concept of rationality from absolute commitment. However, this is not necessary if the role that presuppositions play in all knowledge is appreciated. To talk about presuppositions as foundational to knowledge is to challenge the notion that 'real' knowledge is independent of beliefs. According to the view that I am going to propose, belief and commitment are integral to knowledge of any kind.

Michael Polanyi has probably made one of the most significant contributions to this debate.[2] He was concerned about the assumption, pervading Western thought, that there is a stark contrast between scientific, objective knowledge, and other, more subjective, and therefore less valuable, less trustworthy, forms of knowledge. He sought to challenge this polarization by highlighting the personal nature of scientific enquiry, while still wishing to retain its objective character.

For Polanyi, the clue to understanding science lay in understanding the process of discovery. This is a highly creative and personal act. He cites Einstein's work as the epitome of this, because his discoveries were made 'unaided by any observation that had not been available for at least fifty years before' (1962, page 11). Scientific progress is not, then, a matter of experiments that anyone can perform, but, rather, the outcome of leaps of creative imagination by those who can spot the clues. This is not gambler's luck, but is a natural, insightful ability, a form of wisdom, fostered by training (1962, page 106).

Polanyi argued that passion and commitment are essential components of intellectual life (1962, Chapter 6). These drive scientists on in their mission to discover reality. He regarded Columbus as an exemplar of this committed, intuitive grasping towards an, as yet, hidden reality (1962, pages 277 and 310–11). Risk, daring, and commitment to that which is only partially known, are the characteristics of the scientific endeavour.

One of Polanyi's distinctive contributions lies in his analysis of the nature of these intuitive perceptions. They are part of that knowledge of which we are largely unconscious and yet, which forms the foundation of our thoughts. Most of the time we take them for granted. Polanyi's succinct description of this was that 'we can know more than we can tell' (1967, page 4). He used many illustrations to explain this concept. One of the most telling was of how blind people use a stick as a probe to guide them. The stick becomes an extension of their own body in such a way that they have no conscious awareness of it. Their attention is focused on the new information that the stick is giving about their environment, not on the stick itself. This interiorization, or taking for granted, of the stick is essential if the blind person is to be able to use it effectively. Polanyi described such knowledge as 'tacit'. Other examples he uses are riding a bike, and the anatomical knowledge of an experienced surgeon. In both cases, we rely on subconscious knowledge. Without it, it is impossible to perform effectively at the conscious level.

An important element of this tacit knowledge is what Polanyi calls our 'fiduciary framework' (1962, pages 264–6). By this he means the framework of beliefs, or presuppositions that we have come to hold during our upbringing. I shall call this our 'thinking base'. These beliefs are acquired through membership of particular communities, and it is impossible to escape dependence on them.

Polyani does not see this dependence as something to be regretted. On the contrary, our thinking base is the source of the intuitive inspiration that gives us 'a vision of a solution which looks right and which we are therefore confident to prove right' (1962, page 131). In order to know, therefore, I have to take for granted these beliefs in the same way that blind people take their sticks for granted. Our presuppositions, or thinking base, are the tool that enables us to explore the world. In this sense, belief is essential for any knowledge.[3]

From this reasoning, it becomes ridiculous to maintain that people should hold the central beliefs of their religious faith in a tentative or provisional fashion. To do this amounts to the same as not holding them at all, because it makes them unusable in the development of knowledge. Just as we cannot continually question how we ride a bike if we are to make progress along the road, so we cannot continually question our thinking base if we are to progress intellectually.

If Polanyi is right, it is also unrealistic to maintain that religious belief should be freely chosen without influence from parental, or other upbringing. The truth is that no one can choose their beliefs in this way. Cultural transmission is an essential element in the way we obtain the presuppositions that make thought possible in the first place. In effect, we 'swallow down' (Lloyd, 1986, page 142) these basic beliefs, and this applies as much to the atheist as to the religious person. To seek to be free from this influence is not to be rational. It is, rather, to harbour a Utopian dream that refuses to accept the limitations that exist for us all in being human. We are all products of the particular. Normal rationality is dependent on commitment to beliefs that, to a degree, we have absorbed from others.[4]

Polanyi has, then, examined the structure of scientific knowledge and concluded that it has an important, 'personal' dimension. He was essentially concerned to give permission to the holding of an absolute commitment by showing that it is rational to do so, because without such commitment there can be no knowledge. He wanted to debunk the notion that there are superior, belief-free, forms of knowledge that are objective and public in a way other, purportedly more personal, forms of knowledge, such as religion, are not. Therefore, he is rejecting an ideal of objectivity that seeks to eliminate all prejudice, bias, and conjecture from the act of knowing. So, rationality is not about waiting for adequate evidence before you believe anything. Rather, the presumption is in favour of the *permission* to believe.[5] We can argue, therefore, that individuals have a right to believe. The beliefs they have inherited as part of their upbringing should be treated as innocent until proved guilty, as it were. This is in direct contrast to those writers surveyed in Part I, who see religious belief as rationally dubious when compared with other forms of 'knowledge'. However, if Polanyi is right, absolute commitment to beliefs is not only justified, but essential to the growth of knowledge. I suggest that he is right.

Towards an Alternative View

The Nature of Rational Commitment

ANY DREAM WILL DO?

The main objection to the position outlined in the previous section is that it sanctions all kinds of unreasonable beliefs, simply on the grounds that someone declares them to be fundamental beliefs for them, central to their thinking base. This has been dubbed the 'Great Pumpkin Objection' (Plantinga, 1983, page 74). If belief in God is rational, it is asked, why cannot the belief that the Great Pumpkin returns every Halloween also be rational? In the same way that theists are entitled to claim that they *know* God, even though they cannot convince the atheist of the truth of their belief, it would surely follow that believers in the Great Pumpkin are also entitled to claim they *know* that the Great Pumpkin exists, despite being unable to convince the sceptic?

The reality is, however, that argument and evidence do count in assessing fundamental beliefs; they are not purely arbitrary, simply accidents of our location of birth. Polanyi emphasizes that, although much of our thinking base is transmitted to us in a tacit way, and received on authority, personal knowledge is neither subjective, nor relative. One of the most important passions involved in the search for knowledge is the desire to come into closer contact with reality. The scientist continually experiences a tension between remaining committed to the received thinking base of the scientific tradition, and breaking out from it into new discoveries that may well challenge this tradition. Reality has the potential to surprise us and challenge our cherished beliefs. Polanyi describes the experience in this way:

> Any tradition fostering the progress of thought must have this intention: to teach its current ideas as stages leading on to unknown truths which, when discovered, might dissent from the very ideas which engendered them. (1967, page 82)

Polanyi, therefore, believes that the desire for objectivity is an important characteristic of a rational belief. He recognizes that reality can only be explored from within a framework of beliefs, but, in the final analysis, this can be overthrown by contact with the reality it strives to comprehend. Alvin Plantinga describes the experiences and other beliefs that challenge our own fundamental beliefs in this way as 'potential defeaters'.

Exactly how reality impinges on our beliefs to change them is not made clear by Polanyi. The writings of Imre Lakatos (for example, 1970) provide a helpful additional clarification. Like Polanyi, he argues that our exploration of the world is guided by a framework of beliefs, which he terms a 'research programme'. This is an interconnected set of theories that consists of two components. First, there is a 'hard core' of *non-negotiable beliefs*, those I have, up until now, called fundamental beliefs. These define the central features of a person's understanding of the nature of reality. As such, they constitute the definitive truth claims of a tradition. To make a change in one's hard core is not to experience a development in one's beliefs, but a revolution, or, in religious terms, a conversion. Around this core is a 'protective belt' of ideas, in which the core beliefs are interpreted, developed, and applied. The parallel with Polanyi's work is that, together, the hard core and protective belt make up the *fiduciary framework*.

This brief description implies a more clear-cut distinction between hard core and protective belt beliefs than is actually the case. It is not something that is set in stone, so beliefs can change their status within a belief system, and, yet, the belief system may still maintain its identity. Thus, a belief that was at one time considered to be part of the hard core may become more negotiable, and, therefore, move into the protective belt. An example would be attitudes towards ordaining women priests within the Church of England. Of course, this example also illustrates that what some may now want to treat as a modifiable, protective belt belief, others will want to retain as part of the non-negotiable hard core. In the final analysis, it is these non-negotiables that are the focus of the loyalty which gives people their identity as believers of a particular kind. To totally abandon a hard core is to change one's identity, to be converted. However, to allow traffic between the hard core *and* the protective belt is to seek to develop a more adequate commitment. The debate within the Church of England represents a difference of opinion as to exactly which of these strategies the Church is currently engaged in.

One important insight from Lakatos' theory is his belief that, when a thinking base is challenged by a potential defeater (to use

Plantinga's terminology), abandoning the framework is not the only possible rational response. It is legitimate, for example, to reinterpret the data in the light of one's own beliefs, or to make modifications in your protective belt ideas, so that the hard core is maintained in the face of the potential defeater. The change in Roman Catholic thinking, under the influence of Karl Rahner, from *exclusivism* to *inclusivism* is an example of such a shift.[6] This was a response to the realization that it was simply untenable to go on treating other religions as little more than vehicles of damnation. However, in order to preserve the doctrine of the uniqueness of Christ, believers in non-Christian religions were now to be viewed as 'anonymous Christians'. Thus, there was a shift in Catholic belief about other religions, but one that protected their hard core belief in the uniqueness of Christ as the only means of salvation. Plantinga calls this strategy 'defeating the defeater' (1983, page 84). It entails a process of re-negotiation within a particular framework of commitment.

However, according to Lakatos, this process is only justified if the shifts that are made are 'progressive' in character. By this he means that they have greater explanatory power in the sense that they account more effectively for our experience of the world. In our example of the shift from exclusivism to inclusivism, the extra data accounted for is the experience of finding genuine, and sincere faith in non-Christians. Of course, it may be found that the shifts made to accommodate new knowledge are, to use Lakatos' terminology, 'degenerating'. In other words, it becomes increasingly obvious that they are arbitrary and inadequate. An example might be the attempt by literal creationists to interpret the geological record in terms of a flood affecting the whole earth. It is possible for us to be inside a belief system and yet realize that it is not accounting as well as it should for our experience of the world. We can become deeply unsatisfied with our own attempts at explanation. Reality can kick back from inside theories. It is in this way that a research programme begins to break down.

It needs emphasizing that this process of testing beliefs is usually slow, and rarely, if ever, finally conclusive, in the sense of convincing everyone. For example, John Hick would view the arguments I would put forward to support my belief in the uniqueness of Christianity as degenerating shifts. Not surprisingly, I disagree with him on this. It cannot be denied, therefore, that assessing religious beliefs is a difficult and controversial business. However, the important point is that evidence *does count*. There can be progress as we seek to assess the relative merits of various theories, particularly when they do conflict, and so we can make some judgement as to which is the most successful. Religious belief is not arbitrary.

It must be accepted, however, that the point at which a belief system can be said to be fatally degenerating is a matter of personal opinion. So, some people will go on believing in the face of evidence that others find totally destructive. Such resistance to falsification is not necessarily a sign of irrationality. It certainly would be irrational if the possible impact of potential defeaters was not taken seriously by the believer. The right to believe must be balanced by the duty to face up to potential objections. The rational response to a potential defeater, then, is not simply to shrug it off. However, neither is it to give way at the first sighting.

Basil Mitchell tells a parable (1955, page 103–5) to illustrate this point. This recounts the dilemma of a partisan in an occupied country who meets a stranger claiming to be on the side of the resistance. The partisan is utterly convinced by him. However, the stranger is also, at times, seen to be collaborating with the occupier. The partisan goes on trusting the stranger despite his friends' protestation 'What would he have to do for you to admit he is not on our side?' Mitchell sums up the point of his parable as follows:

> The partisan does not allow anything to count decisively against the proposition 'the Stranger is on our side'. This is because he has committed himself to trust the Stranger. But he of course recognises that the Stranger's ambiguous behaviour does count against what he believes about him. It is precisely this situation which constitutes the trial of his faith. (page 104)

Here, it is the feeling of anguish and incomprehension, finally outweighed by the decision to continue to trust the stranger, that marks out the partisan's behaviour as rational. So, the apparent collaboration is explained by the need for the stranger to be seen to be credible with the enemy, when he is, in fact, acting as an agent. The full force of the stranger's ambiguous behaviour is, therefore, felt and weighed, before the decision to go on trusting is made. The point that Mitchell makes from this is that it is quite rational to go on living by a religious belief, even when we know there are problems with it, if there is no other belief available to us that explains our experience more adequately. The *irrational* response is marked by the refusal to see the challenge as *significant*. *Rational* faith is characterized by the measured decision to go on trusting *despite* the challenge.

So, even when believers encounter what seems to others to be a fatal objection to their belief, they may still be within their rights to go on believing. There are two main reasons for this.

First, it may well be that even though they themselves cannot counter the objection, they are aware that experts can, or even that experts are divided over the effectiveness of the objection. In this case, there is no reason for them to give up their belief, even though they cannot personally answer the objection.

Second, their warrant for accepting the belief may be stronger than the objection. Alvin Plantinga cites the case of Moses and the burning bush (1986b, page 312). Here, the belief that God was speaking to him was experientially so powerful for Moses that it carried more weight than the many apparent objections to its possibility.

In addition, we have also to remember that the duty to face up to potential defeaters is dependent on a person's particular circumstances. Two can be identified as being especially important.

1. Our responsibilities are dependent on the possession of certain intellectual capacities and knowledge. A child, therefore, or a person growing up in a very restricted social environment, is within their rights to believe certain things that an adult or member of an open community may not be within their rights to believe. Highly educated and sophisticated adults who set out to demolish what they see as the naive religious beliefs of children and young people would do well to remember this point. Intellectual bullying is as reprehensible as the playground version.
2. We can only be required to take note of those potential reasons for disbelief of which it is reasonable to expect us to be aware. Thus, the believer does not have to suspend belief simply because some philosopher might, at some stage in the future, come up with some potentially fatal objection to belief, or even

because in the past a significant article has appeared in a learned journal. The believer 'cannot be expected to range over the whole world in search of what *might* inhibit his beliefs. He can be expected to range through his mind however' (Wolterstorff, 1983b, page 174).

The nub of these arguments, then, is that one is within one's rights to hold fundamental beliefs even when potential objections exist. There is, indeed, a duty to take these objections seriously, but theories that outline the duties of some idealized, fully knowledgeable, perfectly rational super-human being are of no use to the teacher and do not reflect the reality of religious believing.

An important conclusion from all this is that differences between the religions are not usually going to be finally resolvable through recourse to evidence and argument. When it comes to religion, the nature of rationality means that there will be many tenable options, not a public, objective consensus. It is a matter on which people may reasonably differ. That is not to say, of course, that all the religions are true; it is quite possible for tenable beliefs to be untrue.

At this point, it may help if I recap on the argument running through this section. The key claim has been that religious beliefs are not arbitrary because they aspire to objectivity by attempting to be accurate descriptions of reality. However, such aspirations are of little use if we have no independent means of knowing that we are in any way accurate in our descriptions. The debate between two people arguing about the length of a ruler that is locked inside a drawer is fruitless unless there is some access to the drawer. Lakatos' idea of progressive and degenerating beliefs systems is one suggestion as to how beliefs get a grip on reality. Progressive systems are in touch with reality in a way that degenerating ones are not. The application of basic logical requirements, such as coherence, consistency, and so forth, is another way of testing religious beliefs.[7] However, in the end, there is no finally conclusive way of demonstrating one belief system to be superior to another. In most cases this is a matter on which rational people will disagree. There will always be a number of tenable belief systems. There is one other way that helps us to judge the accuracy of beliefs in describing religious reality. John Hick has argued that we can judge a religion by the quality of life that results from its practice. So, we can legitimately reject the religions of David Koresh at Waco, Texas, whose followers burned to death, and of Jim Jones, who persuaded a thousand of his disciples to commit suicide, as wrong on the grounds of the tragic consequences that resulted from their practice. Nicholas Wolterstorff argues that we can judge a religious belief by whether or not it promotes 'justice-in-shalom' (1984, Chapters 18 and 19), because it is God's goal, revealed in Scripture, that human beings should live at peace in all their relationships. Religious beliefs that, for example, promote racism, or other forms of oppression can never be regarded as genuine. So, religion can be judged by its results (orthopraxis), because it is inconceivable that a correct description of religious reality (orthodoxy) could promote demonstrably evil consequences.

However, it is important to distinguish Hick's position from the realist one I have been describing. I am arguing for the orthopraxis criterion as one means of judging a religion, but not the only one as it is still conceivable that a religion could both promote orthopraxis *and* be wrong in its description of reality. The point is that it cannot be correct without promoting it. Furthermore, two religions could both promote orthopraxis and yet still conflict in their description of reality. The realist, unlike Hick, does not want to treat them as *both* correct, but, instead, ascertain which is the most accurate description of reality.

ARE THERE ANY FACTS?

These discussions raise the important question of whether or not there are such things as facts. Up to now, I may have been seen to be implying that there is no such thing as a fact independent of a framework of beliefs. However, it is clearly a nonsense to argue that there are not facts of experience that we can all agree on, and that are constant across belief systems. For example, Marxists and capitalists will readily be able to agree on the fact that water and petrol have particular, and very different properties. Anyone trying to deny this will soon find out their error at considerable personal cost. Likewise, people holding very different beliefs rely on the same facts when they fly together in an airplane.

Admitting this, however, is not the same as saying that facts can be of any significance in human thought independently of beliefs. Facts are always embedded in a wider theoretical context that gives them a particular meaning. So, for example, two people studying the structure of a bird's wing may agree on the facts of the bone structure, feather function, and so on, but may fundamentally disagree on the wider significance of these facts. Thus, one regards these structural marvels as clear evidence of a Creator God, while the other may see them as an example of evolution, having developed their present form as a result of chance mutation, and natural selection.

The crucial distinction that is being made here is between the position that maintains that there are facts common to all humanity, on which religions and other theoretical systems provide optional glosses, and my position that maintains that facts cannot exist independently of theoretical systems. As my discussions in Part I have shown, the former has been highly influential in educational theory. Its main tenet is that there is 'a domain of autonomous understanding, free of any commitment to one specific tradition' (Hirst, 1985, page 8). This is taken to be logically prior to all metaphysical beliefs.

It is important to realize that this influential position is not itself independent of metaphysical beliefs. It is essentially a humanist perspective that treats religion as a private, additional, and non-essential commentary on the public facts of human experience. In this case, objectivity is identified as public knowledge independent of any particular controversial beliefs.

The alternative view proposed in this chapter rejects this notion that theory-free facts are of more significance than beliefs. I do accept that there are facts that are part of a shared experience of the world, but I want to make an important qualification. Facts *uninterpreted* by beliefs are of no consequence, they are relatively trivial. What matters is the *significance* we attribute to them, and the purposes for which we use and value them. For example, although people of many different faiths can agree on the details of aircraft technology, they may *use* that knowledge very differently: the Nazi may employ it to benefit the 'master race' and in the implementation of genocide; the Christian missionary will use it to reach people with the Gospel; and the businessman to improve his potential for making a profit. In so far as facts of any import exist, in other words besides relatively trivial statements like 'this is water', they are created by the fact that a number of belief systems overlap in the significance they attribute to a statement. An example would be 'it is wrong to steal', which most belief systems endorse.

So, if we take away the belief systems, the facts (in the sense of significant statements) cease to exist. We can no longer discuss them. To evaluate the significance of a fact of experience we have to draw on a belief system. So, there are no such things as significant facts that have a public, non-controversial authority not enjoyed by any of the beliefs. To seek to avoid controversy by concentrating on so-called facts of human experience is, by default, to impose controversial belief. It is to smuggle in beliefs in the name of objectivity.

One of the mistakes that I see being made in the current emphasis on the spiritual dimension in schools is to treat it as though it is a non-controversial fact of human experience. It is sometimes said if we concentrate on that which binds us together, the spiritual, and leave out that which divides, the religious interpretations of the spiritual, then we have a way forward for schools. To return to my butcher analogy (see page 59), I equate this desire to schew the particular with his claim that he can sell meat, without stocking any particular form of it. However, to begin to use the notion of the spiritual in school we have to interpret and apply it. We cannot avoid setting it within a framework of particular beliefs,[8] and this will always be controversial.

Polanyi explores the significance of the theory-laden nature of facts using the analogy of the operation of a machine (1962, pages 329–31). He grants that, at one level, physicists are able to discuss certain facts in relation to it, for example, the strains on materials that may cause it to break down. However, the operational principles of the machine as a whole have to be explained on a higher level, that of engineering. It is this level that, ultimately, is the most important, because it gives us the total picture and enables us to use the machine purposefully. Religion is one higher level of reality, setting the facts of lower levels in a context of meaning and significance. What I am arguing, therefore, is that, although there is a sense in which we can say there are theory-free facts, they exist on only one level of reality, and a less important one at that. Their meaning and significance is only revealed when they are interpreted at a higher level.

A final point that follows from this discussion is that a belief system is never abandoned simply because it is refuted by 'the facts'; but only when another more progressive system is available to take its place. The inconsistencies of one theory are thrown into sharp relief by the presence of another. If we are dissatisfied with our belief system, but do not know of an adequate replacement, we quite simply have to 'make do' with what we have. We cannot just stop believing *per se* because, as Polanyi has shown, this means that we stop thinking. The defeat of a theory is never a straight battle between simple observation and the theory, but, rather, between two theories offering different interpretations of experience.

THE QUESTION OF TRUTH

I have already noted that both John Hick and Joseph Runzo accept that religious believers regard the language they use as making statements about the nature of reality. Religious people do believe there is a state called heaven, one God called Allah, and so forth. It is this belief that their religion puts them in touch with the truth about reality that is the basis for their absolute commitment. To treat religious language as simply making statements about our own inner state is, therefore, to distort the realist nature of religion for the majority of believers.[9]

We can define realism as the view that 'reality exists independently of our conceptions of it though it may coincide with them' (Trigg, 1980, page 3). Polanyi argues that to be rational is to have a responsibility to this reality, because there is a general connection between reality and what rational people would accept if they had enough evidence. By this he means that, in so far as is possible, we have a duty to ensure that our beliefs match reality. The intellectual passion of scientists drives them to seek to discover this reality as it *really* is. Just as a map is limited in how it can be drawn by the nature of the reality it is seeking to describe, so religious language is limited by the nature of God. As scientific language is the attempt to respond to the nature of the world, so religious language is the attempt to respond to the nature of God. It is this feature that distinguishes personal knowledge from subjectivity.

This same passion also means that, having made discoveries, scientists then hold them, as Polanyi puts it, with 'universal intent'. What he means by this is that, having discovered an aspect of reality, we cannot rest with the notion that it is simply reality for me. His views on this are summarized in the following quotation:

> To the extent to which a discoverer has committed himself to a new vision of reality, he has separated himself from others who still think on the old lines. His persuasive passion spurs him now to cross this gap by converting everyone to his way of seeing things. (1962, page 150)

As we seek to describe reality, therefore, we will find that our descriptions are in conflict with those of someone operating from within a different thinking base. In the same way that different scientific theories will conflict with, and exclude, each other, so, too, will different theologies. What is more, the proponents of these different theories will argue for them with universal intent, staking their absolute commitment on what, at that point in time, seems to be the most adequate description of the reality they seek to comprehend. In the final analysis, having considered the evidence carefully, I must say another belief is wrong if it fundamentally conflicts with my own beliefs. Each of us must stake our life on the truth of the beliefs that structure our thinking. Right and wrong, truth and falsity are issues that cannot be ducked if we are to take rationality seriously. Rationality entails conflicts of beliefs.

As we have seen, some theologians feel that such attitudes have tragic social consequences (see page 85). Their concern is that when people believe they are in touch with ultimate truth, all sorts of social evils are practised against those who disagree with them. On the other hand, it certainly will not solve the problems that conflicts of religious beliefs may create if theologians and educationalists deny the reality of the conflict. This is like telling young lovers that it is quite unhelpful for them to have such strong feelings about each other.

Saying this is not to deny the importance of being concerned about the effects of conflicts of religious beliefs. This is a theme to which I will return later in this chapter. Suffice it to say here that an awareness of the distinction between our own attempts to *describe* reality and the *actual nature* of reality will certainly curb unacceptable behaviour. As Arthur Holmes puts it, 'no self-acknowledged creature can reasonably expect to be like God in knowledge' (1983, page 128). Awareness of this must surely make us humble and underline the importance for all of us of taking a dose of self-suspicion. Knowing that we perceive reality from within our own background and commitment, with all its advantages and disadvantages, is reason for being self-critical if we want a chance of seeing what is actually there. A quotation from Polanyi will sum up this approach to religious belief. 'The principle purpose of this book is to achieve a frame of mind in which I may firmly hold to what I believe to be true, even though I know it might conceivably be false' (1962, page 214). Colin Gunton is making the same point when he writes that 'we have every right to claim to know, even though we are aware of the fact that we may be and often are mistaken' (1992, page 96).

This point can be illustrated by looking at the human relationship of love. For the person in love, it is quite inconceivable that they could fall out of love. It is perfectly rational for them to base their life on this belief so that it is the object of absolute commitment. Indeed, this is the only way in which a secure, long-term relationship can be built. Constant questioning of love is actually destructive of it. At the same time, it is dangerous, and irrational, to take love for granted. Therefore, we must be working constantly to maintain the health of the relationship. Of course, there is always the possibility that the relationship might totally fall apart. So, for example, the evidence that my partner was sleeping with another person would probably convince me that the relationship was degenerating. However, until I am presented with such evidence there is no reason at all for me to live my life in the expectation that I will, one day, be presented with it. Indeed, for the person in love, such a possibility is inconceivable, and rightly so.

It is the same with religious belief. Rational people accept that there is always the possibility that their beliefs could be wrong. So, in principle, all beliefs are revisable, and life has to be lived bearing this risk in mind. This attitude fosters a sense of humility and a concern to be critically open to the potential insights to be gained from encounters with other belief frameworks. Certainly, living in a modern pluralist environment highlights the potential revisability of our beliefs.

However, if asked whether or not it is possible that their fundamental beliefs are *in fact* wrong, believers have to answer in the negative. The reason is that, given their present circumstances and knowledge, this is simply inconceivable. For it to be conceivable, there would have to be a major change in these circumstances. With the knowledge currently available to them, then, religious people are within their rights to live their lives on the basis of an absolute commitment to their beliefs.

Therefore, there is a tension in a rational belief structure, which exists between one's duty to accept the potential revisability of beliefs, the realization of which makes learning from others possible, and the right to hold to the inconceivability of their revision, which provides the bedrock for thought and action in the world. Some beliefs simply *must* be unshakeable for reasoning to take place. The alternative is not openness, but intellectual chaos. This view of rational belief is very different to the sceptical attitude, which demands that *all* beliefs be held tentatively. What I am proposing is an understanding of rational belief that can be described as *truth that listens*.

True for All Religion?

The view I have been describing is called a *critical realist* view of religion. This accepts the incompleteness of our knowledge, but also maintains that we can have access to a reality that exists *independently of human thought*. We explore this reality from within our own commitments, and yet our commitments change in the light of our encounters with reality.

The relationship between faith commitment and knowledge of reality can be likened to the way detectives investigate a crime. Their job is to uncover the reality, namely to discover exactly who committed the crime, and how they did it. However, they cannot do this if they keep a completely open mind throughout their investigations. Having first assessed the evidence, they must come up with an initial idea, an intuition, as to who is the culprit, or at least where to start looking for the culprit. This represents a faith commitment, which leads to certain lines of investigation being pursued and others being ignored. As the case is pursued, the commitment to this initial idea will either strengthen, or be modified in the light of the further evidence that comes to light. The best detective, the Sherlock Holmes of the profession, is the person who has the most accurate insights, who can smell a good lead, and is prepared to pursue it relentlessly, while at the same time is open enough to other contradictory evidence, so that the line of investigation is modified when necessary. As commitment to an intuition is essential to successful detective work, so is faith commitment essential to our coming to know the nature of reality. In our search for true knowledge, we, as human beings, have no option but to act on our faith that our way of thinking about the world, (what I have earlier called a thinking base, see page 77), is superior to the alternatives that are available. I suggest that this view is more adequate than the one I examined in Part I, because it takes the absolute nature of religious commitment seriously, without abandoning the attempt to define criteria of rationality.

Critical realism certainly accounts for what we can call the more traditional forms of religious belief: those that claim to make statements that are true as matters of fact, for example, that there is an existence after death. However, there are other types of religion that do not claim to do this. Within the Christian faith, the radical Christian liberalism I have described earlier would be an example. So how can a person who believes that the worlds' major religions are equally valid, or that religious belief is a consequence of our cultural environment, or even that religious language only describes the inner world of the believer, be said to have an absolute commitment to a particular description of the nature of reality? This is a crucial question, because if we use critical realism in secular education as the basis for our understanding of what it means to be rational, and if radical Christian liberalism does not conform to it, then common schools will have to declare radical Christian liberalism to be irrational. This would be an unacceptable violation of the pluralist principle, because whether radical Christian liberalism is, or is not a rational form of belief, is a matter on which reasonable people can differ. Certainly it is extensively debated in theological tomes.

However, I would wish to claim that radical Christian liberalism does conform to the descriptions of critical realism I have given in two essential ways. First, people who espouse this tradition are committed to its truth, and will view those who disagree with them as mistaken. For example, John Hick is committed to the idea that all religions are valid. This leads him to assert that belief in the uniqueness of Jesus Christ and of Christianity is wrong. In his writings, he actively seeks to persuade others of the correctness of his view. It is one to which he is absolutely committed, and which he holds with universal intent. Indeed, he works very hard to discredit the view that salvation can only come through faith in Jesus Christ.

Second, I would claim that radical Christian liberalism does make claims about the nature of reality. Consider the following quotation: 'neither secular nor religious metaphors are necessarily right or wrong, they are simply vehicles we use to articulate experience' (Hammond *et al.*, 1990, page 125). This is an example of subjectivism, the notion that religious language is purely a description of our inner state. Yet, this is clearly a statement about the nature of religious language. It is telling us that the *reality* is that religious language is not one thing (a description of the world), but is something else (a description of how I feel). This is a truth claim about the true nature of religious language. Those who hold this view invest their energy in persuading their detractors of its truth.

In light of this, we can safely say that critical realism is a secure basis for secular education because it is a description of rational belief that does not arbitrarily exclude views on which reasonable people may differ. The only positions it does exclude are those that refuse to accept that they have faith commitments in a false claim to objectivity, or those that refuse to be open to evidence and argument in the assessment of their commitments. These are both unreasonable, and both lead to totalitarianism.

Three Analogies

A trio of analogies based on the behaviour of different objects in water may help us to understand the various theories about belief structures that have been discussed so far.

First, the form of exclusive, absolute structure that worries many religious educationists can be likened to a steel ball in a pond. This will move around in its environment, but will be totally unaffected by it, and may well damage other objects in the pond. It is unchanging, and unresponsive to influences outside of itself. Belief structures like this can appear to be caught in a time capsule, totally unable to change, and adapt. These can be described legitimately as tribal, fundamentalist, or religionist.

The opposite extreme can be likened to a one-celled lifeform that has no control over its internal fluids. Placed in too dilute a solution, it will simply absorb water until it explodes and ceases to exist. Those who argue that religious belief systems should conform to the objectivity of public knowledge are, in fact, advocating that, like this animal, the believer cannot legitimately seek to maintain a distinct identity.

A rational belief structure can be compared to the way in which the one-cell amoeba responds to its environment. First, it will absorb elements of its environment, both passively, through its surface, and actively, by engulfing food, and other particles. These elements are then incorporated into its own structures. In terms of a theory of knowledge, this can be paralleled with the ability of a belief system to both respond to the developments in knowledge that take place around it, and to actively incorporate insights from other belief systems. However, the crucial feature of this is that the amoeba retains a separate, and distinguishable identity from both its general environment, and those particles it engulfs. That which it absorbs becomes 'amoeba' in identity. In the same way, a Christian, for example, in learning from other belief systems incorporates new insights into a Christian belief structure that are clearly distinguishable from their original source. Elements that, on first glance, seem to be shared, turn out not to be so when examined more closely. For example, both Jews and Christians follow the Hebrew Bible, but they read it in very different ways. For the Christian, it points to Jesus Christ, but it does not do this for the Jew.

Second, although the amoeba actively interacts with its environment and other beings in this environment, there will be certain things it cannot absorb without destroying its own identity. In order to remain true to its own 'amoebic nature', there are, therefore, mechanisms whereby it can reject certain elements that it may have absorbed, including excess water, and foreign matter it cannot digest. Similarly, a rational belief system will discriminate between those beliefs that are different to itself but which it *can* incorporate into its own structures, albeit in a modified form, and still remain true to its own identity, and those it *cannot* incorporate without necessitating a gross distortion of its own nature. For example, a modern liberal would find it difficult to incorporate insights from the philosophy of the kamikaze pilot.

What these analogies capture is the fact that the maintenance of a distinct identity, comparable to an absolute commitment to a belief system, *can* go hand in hand with learning from others.

Implications for Education

These discussions have a number of implications for the task of developing a rationale for modern education in its relationship with religion.

To begin with, it can be agreed that many of the concerns that characterize discussions of religious education conducted in terms of learning sickness are quite legitimate. It is important to be able to distinguish between pathological forms of religious faith, which promote intolerant and totalitarian attitudes, and healthy forms, which demonstrate openness to others. We want to be able to distinguish indoctrination, which disables the believer's ability to think and impedes future learning, from education and nurture, which encourage the development of healthy religious belief. My argument has not been with these aims, but with the *way* in which they have been developed in describing the characteristics of a rational belief structure. An approach to religious education designed to combat learning sickness, but based on the theory of rationality that I have been advancing, would have the following four features.

I: THE RIGHT TO BELIEVE

One characteristic feature of the approach I have been criticizing is an inevitable clash between the rights of parents, or a faith community, to pass on a faith, and the rights of the child to autonomy in the matter of religious faith. It is usually asserted that the right of future adults to choose for themselves is absolute, and that this should not be overridden by the upbringing they experience as children. This attitude is grounded in the assessment that religious belief is 'radically contestable', and the conclusion that, in domains with such doubtful status, but enormous personal influence, individuals should decide for themselves. Furthermore, any commitments made should always be tentative as the evidence available is never enough to justify an absolute commitment. In the final analysis, such ideas set nurture and education in opposition, and result in some educationists treating the activities of believing parents as a threat.

Such polarization, however, is unnecessary. To attempt to marginalize the effects of cultural shaping is, if the arguments of this chapter are correct, like taking away the blind person's stick, and, thereby, removing the one means there is for finding out about the world. The fact that we are products of a culture is exactly what makes it possible for us to begin to construct a personal history. Children, particularly, are quite within their rights to hold their beliefs with absolute commitment as their age and lack of experience mean that it is quite rational for them to adhere to the beliefs they have received from their parents.

In practical terms, this means that the value placed by many educationists on the free choices of private individuals should be replaced by an emphasis on the importance of *valuing* and *building on* the traditions children already have. Nurture will then be recognized as *contributing* to the process of education, rather than being in *opposition* to it (Thiessen, 1987, 1993). Parents and faith communities, then, are not to be treated as a problem for education, but, rather, as providing the basis *necessary* for the growth of religious understanding. Absolute commitment on the part of children should be treated as a *right*, to be respected, *not* as evidence of irrationality.

2: THE DUTY TO BE OPEN

At the same time, it has to be recognized that it is not healthy for anyone to remain absolutely locked within one particular belief system, unable to take seriously arguments that potentially count against it. To set out to achieve such a state is one of the characteristics of indoctrination. In a rational structure, there are not only rights, but also duties that have to be taken seriously. These will be a particular concern for religious education.

In practice, this will require the gradual exposure of children to faiths different to their own so as to encourage them to face the challenges that these pose for them. However, this should not be done with the aim of promoting scepticism, or of relativizing, or even unseating the child's faith. To do this would be to infringe on the child's right to believe. Instead, the teacher's aim should be to promote a more rational approach to faith.

This entails that children should be encouraged to face potential defeaters; they should not be allowed to ignore problems with a shrug of the shoulder. As courage is distinguished from recklessness by a full appreciation of the dangers involved in a course of action, so rational belief is distinguished from irrationality when the challenges to faith are felt.

However, the aim of this exposure should be to build a rationally held faith, not to destroy its content. This can be achieved in two ways.

First, children should be introduced to the strategies by which their own faith community defeats these defeaters. Furthermore, they will need to realize that it is sometimes rational, having faced a potential defeater, to make the decision to go on believing *even though* one cannot personally counter it.

Second, they should be encouraged to see how they can learn from encounters with other faith positions by expanding and adapting their own beliefs. They should understand that this can be done while maintaining the specific identity of one's own faith. It goes without saying that the stereotypes of other faiths we all hold need dismantling if this process is to be effective. We cannot learn from another religion if we are prejudiced against it.

Taking these duties seriously is a risky business. Parents who wish to avoid these risks by insisting that their children are only taught one faith with none of its difficulties being addressed, are not facing up to the facts of life. If we wish our children to be mature believers, with a faith that will not collapse when tested by the trials of life, it is important that they are taught to fulfil their duties. In our modern, plural, secular world, challenges to faith cannot be escaped. If children are *not* helped to face them in their formative years, the dangers of either a retreat into ideological enclosure, or radical disillusionment as adults are very real.

Schools are uniquely placed to encourage children to face these challenges. However, this must be done in a way that honours the child's *right* to believe. This can only be achieved if the idea that a mature religious faith is one that is freely chosen and held tentatively is abandoned. This is the influential understanding of autonomy. It needs to be replaced by the notion of responsible self-determination. This entails that each one of us needs to take our responsibility for owning and developing the beliefs that shape us seriously.

3: A BASIS FOR RESPECT

As we have seen, a widespread belief among educationists is that absolutist religious belief systems, which emphasize commitment to truth, are inevitably intolerant, whereas relativist ones are not. I have challenged this assumption by arguing that *all* belief systems, even relativist ones, have limits to their toleration of other beliefs.

However, the theory of knowledge outlined in this chapter does give a firm basis for respecting the rights of others to believe differently to ourselves. Therefore, it provides a platform on which good community relations can be built. It achieves this in two main ways.

First, I have pointed out that the structure of rational religious belief means that there is a pluralism of tenable beliefs, of which mine is one. No finally conclusive way of deciding between these exists. This provides a basis for respecting the right of others to hold beliefs different to my own. For, if I wish to assert my right, on the basis of the pluralist principle, to have my beliefs respected in common schools, I cannot then deny this right to someone else without undermining my *own* demand.

However, this may seem to be a somewhat negative support. A more positive basis for respect presents itself when it is realized that, in order to fulfil our own duties, we actually need proponents of other belief systems to present us with potential defeaters. Thus, interfaith contact is a positive thing as it makes possible my own growth as a believer. Respect for different viewpoints arises from the concern for truth, and the humility that is grounded in a recognition of the fact that I can only reach out towards this by learning from others. This is a far more secure base for good community relations than some romantic, unrealistic notion that differences of religious belief can be absorbed by one, global, unifying theology.

My attitude to the fact of religious pluralism in society must, therefore, be distinguished from the pluralist one. In this case, the argument is that no religion can legitimately claim to be exclusively true, dismissing others as false. Evangelism is interpreted as arrogance, the manifestation of a threatened tribal identity. In contrast, my position is that each one of us is justified in holding our beliefs with universal intent, and that it is rational, therefore, to seek to persuade others of the truth of our position. This is not to deny that we have much to learn from others as we seek to persuade, but is a rejection of the 'I'm only here to learn, not persuade' model of dialogue. I am, in fact, arguing that respect for others is more likely to be found in the believer who has an open, but absolute commitment, than in someone who believes that only a pluralist theology can enable us to respect others.[10]

4: A FURTHER IMPLICATION OF THE PLURALIST PRINCIPLE IN EDUCATION

I argued that the theories of education surveyed in Part I are themselves expressions of particular religious beliefs. For example, the belief that religious language is no more than an expression of deep human emotion is based on a particular understanding of the function of this language. This is no more tenable than the belief that religious language is propositional, making statements about reality. Similarly, the notion that all religions are adequate, complementary references to the same ultimate reality is derived from the belief that God is present in all religions. Again, this is no more tenable than the belief that God was uniquely revealed in Christ, and so on. The clash between modern religious education theory, as outlined in Part I, and more absolutist beliefs is not, therefore, between an irrational approach and a rational approach (as the learning sickness model suggests), but between two approaches, which are both rational *and* tenable, but based on mutually exclusive beliefs. In order to uphold the pluralist principle, *both* should have permission to contribute to education.

A Final Remark

In this chapter, the possible outline of a more adequate theory of religious knowledge has been sketched. It has been suggested that this reflects the actual way in which religious belief is held, and gives a foundation for distinguishing between the rational and the irrational. It can, therefore, form the basis for an approach to religion in schools that both honours the pluralist principle, and accommodates concerns to combat learning sickness. In order to establish its adequacy, it is now necessary to turn to a consideration of how it is to relate to educational principles.

—

CHAPTER SEVEN

Relating Theology and Education
—Towards a New Model

Introduction

IF MY ARGUMENT so far is correct, it seems to leave us with a major problem, which is that it gives little basis for a system of education for all in the plural society. The difficulty is this. I have been proposing that everyone, whatever their religious, or non-religious commitment, has to build their educational values on presuppositions. In other words, education cannot be religiously neutral. It seems, therefore, that it is something that can only take place within 'faith' communities where particular beliefs are shared. Of course, which faith system we choose to underpin education is optional. It is quite coherent to think of Buddhist, Islamic, Christian, and Humanist systems of education. The list is as long as the many thousands of religious traditions that exist in the modern world. However, we cannot escape the fact that presuppositions are foundational to educational thinking.

There seems, therefore, to be little hope of a consensus approach for the common school being developed in a way that will satisfy the various 'faith communities', and, thereby, achieve 'diversity within unity'. The fact is that their various educational 'philosophies' are often in conflict with each other. Indeed, one of the main purposes of this book has been to argue that the modern liberal approach is profoundly antagonistic to more traditional forms of Christian (and other) belief. In this situation, the only option for traditional Christians appears to be to seek to establish schools that are built on educational values derived from their own theology. There are currently two influential attempts to develop this strategy.

The first is to set up independent, distinctively Christian schools for the children of Christian parents, and others who may wish to send their children to such establishments. These are to be distinguished from the Church schools that are part of the State's provision.[1] There is, now, a large number of such schools with a well-established network. Often, they have been viewed with considerable suspicion by those involved in mainstream education. The concern has been twofold. First, there are anxieties that such schools are divisive, and, second, many feel that they are indoctrinatory hothouses. Personally, I feel that these criticisms are more often based on an ideological hostility to confessional, faith-based education than on hard evidence (see pages 24–28). As long as the schools are serious in their concern to avoid indoctrination and tribalism, I can see no reason for them not being a welcome addition to the spectrum of educational provision. However, they are not the concern of this book.[2] I shall, therefore, turn to the second strategy, which focuses on common schools.

This second option rests on the view that Britain is essentially a Christian country. Surveys showing that the majority of people in Britain see themselves as Christian are quoted extensively by supporters of this position. Added fuel for their case comes from the fact that adherents to non-Christian religions form a small minority in modern society. If State education cannot escape having a religious value base, then, it is argued, this should surely be the one shared by the majority of its citizens, and that has shaped the institutions of the nation. As one commentator expressed it, 'The church has profoundly influenced the lives of Britons for fourteen centuries . . . That is why experience of the established church should surely be part of every British schoolchild's education' (Elkin, 1992).

Lady Olga Maitland summed up the argument when, in a speech in the House of Commons, she said, 'The time has come to stop being apologetic about being a Christian country. We should not allow non-believers to undermine our traditions' (*Christian Herald*, 1992).

The key difficulty with this position is that it does not recognize that religion is a matter on which people may reasonably differ. Its proponents assume that it is legitimate to propagate the traditional Christian perspective through common schools. The State is deemed to have the right to impose the 'truth'.[3] However, they are not usually happy when Islamic, or atheistic regimes use similar arguments. Nor is this group happy about the increasing influence of secular humanism or New Age thinking, currently both very popular belief systems, in modern schools. They ignore the fact that, whatever sentimental attachments people may express in surveys, most people in modern Britain are not active Christians. A visit to the local newsagent will demonstrate this fact; it is the *Sunday Sport* that is stocked, not the *Methodist Recorder*. In the final analysis the proponents of this view are seeking to protect *their* version of Christianity by propagating it through schools, ignoring its controversial status, and the pluralism that exists both within and without the Church. One Christian writer illustrated this attitude when he wrote 'Education is the high ground in the Christian's battle with the forces of humanism and atheism' (Perks, 1992, page 9). For him, it is treason against God for Christians to hand children over to be educated 'by our enemies' (page 30). Understandably, other groups feel very threatened by this approach, and react by seeking the power to propagate *their* 'truth'. So, schools become ideological battlegrounds between different groups engaged in gladiatorial contests to try and gain the upper hand. Not a good prognosis for a mixed society.[4]

This all seems very bleak, but there is a way forward. It entails a revision of our attitude to the status of education. Traditionally, we have viewed it as the promotion of that which is of ultimate value for human beings. In other words, we instinctively feel that education should promote values that offer absolute definitions of the good life. Influential examples of people who take this view are Paul Hirst, who fleshed it out in terms of the nature of rationality, and Michael Grimmitt, who uses the concept of humanization. As we have seen, however, their conclusions are unacceptable to more traditional religious believers. So, these believers, in turn, argue that their ideal values ought to form the framework of education, for example, 'the Judaeo–Christian–Islamic beliefs in God, man's accountability to God and the afterlife' (Ali Ashraf, 1988, page 71) or 'God-given moral absolutes for personal and social conduct' (Burn and Hart, 1988, page 31). The problem is that people differ fundamentally on what is the ideal, the good life that should be pursued. Education is, then, always linked to particular interpretations of this. So, it is this idealistic view of education that has to change if we are to achieve 'diversity within unity'.

Another View of Education

Instead of treating education as some universal concept intrinsically linked to idealized values like rationality and truth, I suggest it should be seen as a process designed to fulfil the learning needs of people in a particular context.

Recent discussions of the relationship between religion and education have arisen within a very particular context. Grimmitt describes this as ' "study" in the State school context' (1981, page 46) and Hull as 'a public activity of the State' (1984, page 223). It is not surprising, then, to find that the majority of the literature on this issue in Britain concentrates on developing an approach to religious education that is appropriate for common schools; it is addressing a very specific situation. From now on, I shall call this type of education 'schooling' to distinguish it from that form of education appropriate to faith communities, namely 'nurture'. My comments in the rest of this chapter are concerned with schooling, in this sense, and how it can accommodate the religious dimension.

One essential feature of schooling is that it must be appropriate for all citizens. As we have seen (see pages 69–71), it is widely accepted that, in a democratic society, this must be based on 'the pluralist principle of respect for diversity in areas of belief where people may reasonably differ' (Crittenden, 1988, page 126). The adjective generally used to describe this type of State function is *secular*, which encapsulates the rejection of a totalitarian, or paternalist role for the State in favour of one where its function is 'to be impartial amongst various religious groups in every way' (Storkey, 1979, page 311). The role of the State is 'the impartial administration of social justice' (McCarthy, *et al.*, 1981, page 155). This is to support a view of democracy that does not give the majority the right to ride roughshod over the minority. Rather, the State is responsible for the promotion of principles such as peace, impartiality, and tolerance. Furthermore, the State's sphere of influence is regarded as limited, so that it has no right to control, for example, family life, or the life of a religious community, except in so far as it is protecting individuals from the criminal activities of others. This is an approach that seeks to maximize freedoms, and minimize impositions.[5]

From this viewpoint, the function of the State is to produce a middle ground 'where people from various faiths can transact their business and engage in dialogue, protected by the freedoms associated with democratic government' (Hill, 1985d). Schooling is part of this middle ground, where the State has a legitimate, but limited, role to play in ensuring that children are prepared for their role as citizens. We can say, therefore, that, in schooling, the role of the State is to promote the common good in a way that ensures justice both for individuals *and* for faith communities, as well as meeting the needs of society as a whole. Put another way, it is to ensure that members of society are religiously educated in such a way that they are enabled to function as responsible citizens in the plural context. This should be carried out so that no one's rights, in the matter of religious belief, are violated. Christians cannot, then, simply assume that activities and goals appropriate to education in churches are also appropriate for State schools.

I suggest that there are two features of citizenship that are appropriate concerns for secular schools. In discussing these, I shall attempt to develop an understanding of the secular realm that promotes fairness, while also respecting the integrity of the religions.

I: COMMUNITY HARMONY

There can be little doubt that one responsibility of the State is to ensure that the competing belief systems in society do not become a source of danger to either individual citizens, or to society as a whole. An important function of State schooling, therefore, will be to promote peaceful coexistence between different faith communities. This will entail encouraging those of differing commitments to learn to work together towards the achievement of the common good. In some cases, this will require a change of attitude away from conflict and suspicion, and towards co-operation and joint action. This is essential because, in the words of Hans Küng, 'peace among the religious is a prerequisite for peace among the nations' (Browning, 1990, page 341). Put simply, schooling will have the aim of promoting friendship (Browning, 1990) by encouraging children to reflect on how those of fundamentally different beliefs can embark on joint action to create community in the context of plurality.

Achieving these goals will entail teaching what has been called the *skill of conversation* (Aspin, 1988, pages 45 and 48; Totter-dell, 1988, page 48; Jones, 1987, pages 54–5; Jackson, 1992). In this, children learn to understand and interpret the position of others as well as to understand and explain their own deeply held beliefs. This skill is essential if children are to be able to co-operate with others in the common enterprise of creating a harmonious society. To teach the skill of conversation, then, is to teach children to appreciate the structure of religious belief, and the way in which it is held. The goal is that they begin to explore the impact of belief in their own lives, and those of others, and to learn how to build strategies for co-operative action with others. To teach conversation is to attack one dangerous source of cross-cultural misunderstanding—the fact that many of our most fundamental beliefs are held in a tacit, unconscious fashion. To teach the skill of joint action is to encourage children to find ways in which their beliefs overlap with those of someone else, who may differ radically from them, so that both, with integrity, may participate in the common enterprise of building community. Children will then discover that those holding fundamentally different beliefs have common interests that can form the basis of a co-operative enterprise (Hulmes, 1989, page 148).

What I am suggesting is very different to asserting a universal, educationally acceptable theology to which all are expected to subscribe in the name of tolerance. Rather, schooling is the process of promoting conversation and co-operative action. This has to take on board the various theologies that exist in the particular market-place it serves. It cannot be treated as having some ideal, independent rationality to which all participants have to subscribe. As one writer expressed it:

> Educational practice now becomes not a battle for the minds and hearts of children but as that form of morally committed human intercourse which seeks to bring about and sustain an interplay, or more modestly perhaps, to get it under way in some minimal and genuine way. (Hogan, 1990, page 23)

One of the objections to this approach is that it entails an unrealistic faith in the ability of schooling to act as a form of social glue, or a panacea for society's ills. As someone who objects strongly to the moral decline of the nation being blamed on teachers and schools, I have a lot of sympathy with this argument. I, too, despair when politicians and others seem to assume that if schools only taught children the Ten Commandments, somehow vandalism and hooliganism would disappear from our streets. However, it is a mistake to overreact to this simplistic assessment by arguing that schools have *no* influence on the values imbibed by their pupils. Schools *do* have to make a choice as to whether they are going to throw in the towel in the face of social pressures, or seek to play a transforming role in society, despite the difficulties. If the conclusion reached was that increased understanding is of no greater value than ignorance in children's attitude development, it would be a very dark day for schooling. It would be an irresponsible government that did not seek to promote attitudes of responsible citizenship through its schools. Of course, a sober view of the relative importance of other social influences besides schooling has to be made, and some of the more Utopian educational dreams rejected. Other institutions in society, not least the Church, must also be actively investing in influencing the minds and hearts of young people. However, to dismiss the role of schooling as a force in shaping future attitudes is to dismiss the rationale for much of what happens in education. Teaching children the skill of interfaith conversation is both a proper, and an important concern for State schooling.

2: RATIONAL BELIEVING

A second requirement that State schooling can reasonably make of its pupils in fulfilling its role of preparing young people for citizenship, is that religious beliefs are held in a rational way. What is meant by this in relation to religious belief was discussed at length in Chapter 6, so, here it will suffice to indicate briefly just two features of rational believing.

First, children should be encouraged to consider evidence, and engage in debate with others as important ways of discovering truth. Encouraging this is to value individual self-determination, in the sense that each person takes responsibility for the beliefs that shape them. This is not to imply that *everyone* will reach the *same* conclusions, but to affirm that schooling is concerned with the pursuit of truth. The health of a plural society depends on its various faith groups accepting the importance of debate, and discussion. This will entail both presenting our own point of view, and listening carefully to the views of others. Only with this attitude is conversation possible.

Second, part of being rational in relation to religion is to respect the right of other people to hold beliefs different to our own. We expect our beliefs to be respected, so we should accord the same respect to others. This is to accept the fact that religion is a matter on which people may reasonably differ. There are many tenable religions and it is the job of secular schools to help children understand this fact. This should not, of course, be done in a way that implies that truth does not matter. Nor should we hide the conflicts that exist between the beliefs of the different religions. However, we do need to teach children to accept pluralism as a fact of life, for the sake of the health of our plural society.

The secular State, therefore, has a legitimate interest in promoting, through its schools, rationality in these two senses. They are part of what it means to be a responsible citizen. However, this is a strictly limited interest, and should not spill over into favouring any one view of what the truth might be. The mistake of many liberal educators is to have done just this.

Education and Coalition

The view of education that I am proposing emphasizes the importance of taking into account the context that it is serving. Common schools operate within quite rigid strictures, derived from the limited, secular responsibilities of the State in relation to religious belief. Any theology wishing to interact with State schooling has to be able to accept that the situation presents certain givens because it has to be appropriate for, and serve the needs of, all citizens. All believers have ambitions for society as a whole, which arise from their personal theologies because beliefs are held with universal intent. Although in a democratic society it is quite acceptable that these should be pursued through persuasion of others, certain restraints on these aspirations will have to be accepted to be able to engage in schooling as an activity of the State. Here, education has to operate on the principle of coalition, which the *Shorter Oxford English Dictionary* defines as 'a temporary alliance of distinct parties for a limited purpose'. In order to be able to participate in a coalition, we have to accept certain limitations on our personal ambitions, and negotiate common goals with those with whom we may differ quite fundamentally.

THE DANGER OF COMPROMISE

The problem for many Christians is that they see such negotiation as compromise. Terry Lewis, a Christian education consultant in Canada, captures this concern in a parable that he tells:

> A bear hunter came upon a bear calmly eating berries. As he took aim, he stepped on a twig. The sound alerted the bear, who looked up and saw the gun.
> 'Stop!', the bear cried. 'Why do you want to shoot me? I'm just out to have a meal. Can't we sit down and discuss this?' Being a reasonable, well-educated, civilized man, and also curious about the bear's ability to speak, the hunter accepted the animal's invitation. Sitting down, he told the bear he was hunting because he wanted a fur coat. The bear said that all he wanted was a meal. Soon, bear and hunter were deep in discussion about finding compromises to solve the problem. Sure enough, a compromise was found. The bear had his meal and the hunter was inside his fur coat. (Lewis, nd)

For Lewis, the moral of the story is that negotiation can be deadly. It is most certainly true that, in engaging in joint action with those of other faiths, there is always the danger that we compromise our own position, and damage our integrity. It is said that a frog placed in dangerously hot water will immediately leap out. However, one that is placed in cold water that is gradually heated up to the same temperature will be boiled alive without protest. The *gradual* nature of the change means that it does not notice the threat. The point is that immersion in a situation of interfaith co-operation may threaten our own beliefs without *our* noticing it.

Certainly, some religious educators seem to feel that we should be willing to sacrifice even our most fundamental beliefs in the cause of harmony. Thus, Malcolm Jones writes that 'compromise in the interests of social stability is the rational course and it is a respectable aim in education' (1987, page 54). In his discussion, he treats religious belief as a purely cultural phenomenon, and sees problems in education as arising from 'positive prejudice in favour of the traditions of our home culture' (page 48). In his view, such prejudice is understandable as it is the human emotional attachment to a way of life in which we feel at home. However, it is quite irrational to assert it as unquestionably true, and to be unwilling to abandon such sentimental attachments for the higher good of social cohesion. Such lack of concern with truth, though, does not take seriously the nature of religious belief, and is quite unacceptable to many faith communities. Like John Hick, Jones resorts to trying to revise the nature of religious belief in the cause of harmony, regarding it as nothing more than understandable prejudice for our home culture. He fails to appreciate that there is more to the fear of compromise than a simple distaste for another person's culture, and a fear of being contaminated as a result of contact with it.[6] There is also the question of loyalty to truth.

I suggest that we need to distinguish between *compromise*, and what I shall call *restraint*. Compromise implies abandoning that which is fundamental, and is certainly a word with negative overtones for many people. It also has the connotation of something that can happen to us unwittingly. We speak of being compromised, rather like the frog caught unawares by the gradually rising temperature of the water; it is not something we agree to, or are in charge of. Restraint, however, suggests that we are prepared to accept what is the second best as far as our own beliefs go, because it is recognized that good ends can be achieved through such action. It is active, something we decide to do. It means refraining from insisting that our own beliefs should be normative in the public context because it is appreciated that to do so may have unjust consequences for those who do not share our beliefs. It means being able to accept different goals for different situations, and not insisting that our own theological first principles are applied, irrespective of the context. I will illustrate what this might mean in practice for one religious tradition in Part III.

TWO IMPORTANT PRINCIPLES

There are two key factors that are integral to the success of any coalition. First, the limited purposes that are being pursued through any particular coalition must be fully understood by all those involved. Second, there has to be a clear understanding of how the differences between the various parties involved are to be handled; procedural rules of behaviour have to be established. British parliamentary democracy is an example of such a coalition. In this case, the limited purpose to be achieved is that the nation is governed in a way that is efficient, but which minimizes injustice, and maximizes accountability. In order to be able to function within this structure, individuals and parties have to accept that there are certain rules of procedure that govern the way the very fundamental differences of belief represented within the Houses of Parliament are to be managed. These rules act as a restraint on the pursuit of the political ideal as viewed from any particular party perspective.

The rules are themselves *impartial*—in the sense that they are not derived from the beliefs of one particular political party— but they are far from *neutral*, because they are underpinned by certain values about how deep differences of political belief should be handled in the public context. The rules are open to future modification, of course, but, if anyone wants to participate in government, then they are bound to accept them at that time, with the consequence that they may be severely limited in the realization of their own ambitions. For example, at the time of writing, Liberal Democrats have to work with a 'first past the post' system, and be committed to operating the rules associated with this system, even though they would rather have a system of proportional representation. (Of course, they also seek to use the opportunities present within this system to transform it into the one they would prefer.) Therefore, there is a price to be paid for participating in public political activity.

The interaction of religion and education in the public context of schools provided by the State can be viewed in a similar way. Such a situation requires that a coalition be established between the various faith groups in society, and that the limited purposes of schooling in this context be clearly identified. The statement produced by the Association of Religious Education Advisers and Inspectors is a model of the sort of purposes that could be pursued. It said that the aims of religious education are three-fold:

To help a pupil to explore religion in order to achieve knowledge and understanding of religions, their beliefs experiences and practices;

To contribute to the development of a pupil's own beliefs and values;

To encourage a pupil to respect the rights of others to hold beliefs different from their own. (1989, page 5)

These enshrine the two goals of State religious education that were discussed earlier, namely the promotion of harmonious relationships between citizens of different religious persuasions, and the promotion of rationality in the way people hold their religious beliefs. They are limited goals in that they do not embrace the nurture of children within, or attempt to win children's allegiance to, any specific faith commitment. They are, therefore, not *confessional*. In principle, any faith community should be able to accept them without threat as long as they can accept the importance of promoting community harmony, and the view of rational belief I have put forward. However, if teachers go beyond these, and attempt to evangelize children, or deconstruct their beliefs, they have destroyed the potential for coalition, and violated the pluralist principle.

The second requirement for a successful coalition is a clear understanding of how the deep differences between members are to be handled. This means that certain 'rules of engagement' have to established that will govern the behaviour of all who are to be participants in the co-operative activity of schooling. These would form the basis of a code of conduct, which would act as articles of peace for the various groups involved, rather than articles of faith to which all are expected to subscribe. Such an approach is being developed in the context of interfaith dialogue (CCIFR, 1993), and models are available in educational literature from India (for example, Tluanga, 1989, pages 64–76). Two examples from current British literature will serve to illustrate the point.

First, it is now widely accepted that responsible religious educators employ 'owning' and 'grounding' language (Read, *et al.*, 1992, pages 67–8). By this is meant that all statements of belief are owned by a particular individual (for example, the vicar who comes in as a visitor to an RE lesson), or grounded in particular faith communities. So, phrases like 'as a Christian, I believe . . .', or 'Orthodox Christians believe that . . .', are preferred to one like 'thinking people no longer believe . . .'. The purpose of utilizing this style is to avoid compromising both pupil and teacher by assuming, or seeking to coerce, their assent to certain propositions by using inclusive language.

A second example comes from the resource pack called *The Gift to the Child*, developed at Birmingham University. Here, it is suggested that, in using religious material with young children, there should come a point at which a 'distancing device' is introduced into the lesson (Grimmitt, *et al.*, 1991, pages 10–11). The purpose of this is to create a boundary that most of the children may not cross. The aim is that children clearly distinguish religious material that does not belong to them from that which does. So, for example, the only children allowed to share food dedicated to Ganesh are those who actually belong to the Hindu community. To achieve the same effect, the project also produced a series of books, with photographs of a child belonging to a faith community involved in the practices of that community. This enables particular religious material to be spoken of in the third person, as belonging to, for example, the Sikh boy Sabjit (page 51), and avoids giving the impression that all the class are expected to believe it.

The important point to note about *any* educational code of conduct developed under this model is that it cannot be treated as representing a publicly approved theology, a basis of faith to which all are expected to subscribe. Rather, it is pragmatic agreement that makes partnership possible. It would be a nonsense, therefore, to seek to apply it in situations outside of the context for which it was developed, for example, within faith communities.

A Return to the Idea of the Secular

Central to this discussion of the relationship between theology and education has been the concept of secularity. Those writing from the professional standpoint argue that education must be secular if it is to fulfil the needs of the plural society. Those writing from the religious perspective reject this as an imposition of the anti-religious framework of secular humanism. Lesslie Newbigin has addressed this issue at some length in his writings. He picks up both these concerns in the following extract:

> Especially in a country like India, long riven by interreligious tensions and struggling to create a single, strong nation, the vision of a genuinally secular society was and is compelling. Such a society, it was believed, would provide free space for the exercise of religion. It would not be in any sense antireligious. It would safeguard the freedom of each person to follow the religion of his or her choice. But it would not allow any particular religious belief to govern national policy or have a privileged place in education. This has been, and is, the hope of many devoutly religious people. But beyond this, and especially in the so-called developed world, there has been and is a further expectation—namely that the process of secularization would inevitably lead to the gradual disappearance of religious belief, that secularization is an irreversible process, and that the farther society moves along the road of rationalization, and urbanization, the more certain it is that religion will have a receding role in society. (1989, page 212)

Newbigin's main objection is that the result of this drift from the first to the second sense of 'secular', has been to deny the Christian Gospel its role as public truth. Furthermore, it has anaesthetized Christians into accepting that the 'reigning plausibility structure' (his name for a thinking base) of Western liberalism provides an objective, superior intellectual vantage point. They have been coerced into treating this as providing the absolute, authoritative basis for public values. It seems to me that the attempt to generate educational principles that are independent of religious belief is to do just this. For Newbigin, the Gospel should not be privatized in this way. The role of the Church is to challenge this dominant plausibility structure.

A central argument in this book is that there is a slide in many writings on schooling from an acceptance of Newbigin's *first* sense of the secular, with its vision of the just society, into the *second*, which excludes most theology from public life. As we have seen, a further significant drift in this process is to view that which is secular as superior to that which is religious. The following quote from Michael Grimmitt illustrates this attitude:

> The value ascribed to being sensitive, respectful, thoughtful, open-minded, empathetic and tolerant towards a faith other than one's own and appreciative of diversity of belief is not derived from the religions. Even though each religion may teach that human life is to be valued and respected, no religion advocates that human beings should be open-minded with regard to the beliefs they hold—if they did, current tensions between the religions and education would not exist. Although religions bind people of common faith together, they also divide them from people who believe differently; one cannot believe in more than one religion because each offers beliefs which are mutually exclusive. So the values of tolerance towards, and appreciation of diversity are not, for the most part, religious values; they are educational values. (1991, page 81)

The surprising thing is that this anti-religious conclusion has been reached in the attempt to find a rationale for education that is appropriate for the multifaith society; a rationale that, it is claimed, is secular in Newbigin's first, impartial sense; although the reality is that it is secular in the second sense. In contrast, I believe a viable approach to schooling can *only* be built on a position that remains *consistently* secular in this first sense. To do this, it must emphasize fairness, and resist the drift into the second, superior sense.

Probably the single most important step in remaining true to the impartial ideal is to break the link between the notion of the secular and the idea that knowledge is independent of religious belief. I have already argued at length that all knowledge is embedded within a framework of beliefs. For educationists to argue otherwise results in the imposition of a particular belief framework because they think that they have succeeded in the alchemists' quest of isolating this objective knowledge. However, in arguing this, I am not rejecting the notion of secular knowledge altogether. We have seen that different belief frameworks can, and do, overlap with each other. This is particularly so when different faith groups are living together in a plural community. It is this overlapping of belief systems that produces secular knowledge, creating a sort of neutral middle ground.

The fundamental distinction between the two ideas of the secular can be illustrated by considering different attitudes to the use of religious language in the secular educational context. In the second, anti-religious sense, to speak as a Christian in a discussion on the aims of religious education would be seen to be quite inappropriate. However, from the point of view I am proposing, it is recognized that a person's religious beliefs are not simply an appendage to secular educational values that should be left out of the debate. On the contrary, they provide the rationale, and justification for these values. The reason many Christians feel that it is important to work in common schools is very much to do with their belief in God. To talk of this as a Christian vocation is, then, quite appropriate. It is my Christian convictions that make the promoting of community harmony important for me. For humanists, it will be their humanist convictions. There are not some compelling, rational principles that are independent of, and superior to, these faith-based values. What makes schooling a *secular* activity is that it is seen to be important by a number of belief systems. At this point, their ideals overlap, although they will root them in very different beliefs. In terms of a public education policy, a shared concern for community harmony generated by the overlapping of the belief systems can provide a platform for co-operative action. However, the different and particular beliefs underlying this shared concern in each case cannot be part of public policy as the authority of a particular theology is internal to the faith community that shares it. No one theology, therefore, can be public in the sense of providing the value base for a coalition enterprise sponsored by the State in a plural democracy.

If it is accepted that secular education is made possible because certain goals can be shared as a result of the overlaps between belief systems being great enough to allow a common enterprise to proceed, then it can be seen that a number of different theologies will be playing an adjudicating role in justifying secular education.[7] Thus, there will be Humanist, Christian, Islamic, and so on, rationales for the *one* process of secular education. Each rationale will be internal to its own presuppositions, but the overlaps between them will provide the basis for a common approach to schooling for all. There is not, however, some independent, logically superior rationality that is *more* objective than any of these contributing theologies, and, so, in authority over them.

Secular education, therefore, is the result of different faith groups coming together to form a coalition. The partners in the enterprise will have to regard a co-operative approach to schooling in the plural society as a worthwhile activity. This is more likely to be so if the fact that such schooling can only have limited purposes is respected, and a clear code of conduct is established as to how the differences that exist between the partners are to be handled. Therefore, educational ideals appropriate to the faith community context *cannot* be pursued in the secular context, and this will have to be accepted by all involved. So, one important element in the code of conduct will be the willingness to exercise restraint in pursuing otherwise legitimate theological ambitions, particularly the understandable desire to apply them with universal intent. Co-operation, then, *is* possible at a practical level in the secular educational enterprise, although agreement on its justification is not. Diversity within unity is achieved not by denying that diversity in the name of some objective secular ideal, but by pointing to the potential for co-operation between those of different beliefs in the achievement of limited, but theologically worthwhile, secular goals.

A quotation from Jacques Maritain will act as a suitable summary for this section:

> I am fully convinced that my way of justifying the belief in the rights of man and the ideals of liberty, equality, fraternity, is the only one which is solidly based on truth. That does not prevent me from agreeing on these practical tenets with those who are convinced that their way of justifying them, entirely different from mine, or even opposed to mine in its theoretical dynamism, is likewise the only one that is based on truth. Assuming they both believe in the democratic charter, a Christian and a rationalist will nevertheless give justifications that are incompatible with each other, to which their souls, their minds and their blood are committed, and about these justifications they will fight. And God keep me from saying that it is not important to know which of the two is right! That is essentially important. They remain, however, in agreement on the practical affirmation of that charter, and they can

formulate common principles of action. (Guinness, 1991, pages 43–4)

The Responsibilities of the Professional Teacher

One of the challenges for anyone seeking to relate theology and secular education is to define the principles that should govern the professional behaviour of the theologically committed teacher. John Hull is anxious that this is done in a way that avoids 'relegating the personal religious faith of the teacher to the private sphere' (1980a, page 1). Amen, I say! He commends the approach of what he calls the 'divergent' teacher, who is someone willing to teach beliefs different from their own. A divergent teacher is secular in our first, impartial sense of the word. In other words, this is someone who supports the pluralist principle, despite holding their own theology with universal intent. So, to be professional is to respect the fact that education in the secular context must be limited in its aims. It is to be committed to working within the area of overlap of the various belief systems. Professional teachers are, then, those who are prepared to enter into coalition with others, who accept the constraints of the State-sponsored educational context, and who are willing to abide by the code of conduct appropriate to this context. They are people who respect the norms appropriate to the secular classroom.

However, to be professional should not be linked to accepting secular educational principles as our *first order commitment*, taking precedence over our personal theological commitment. This could only be justified if educational principles were taken to be superior to theological ones. In fact, the opposite is true. Our acceptance of secular educational principles is grounded in our personal theology. Commitment to professional values, then, is dependent on, not independent of, particular faith commitments. The only way in which professional values can be said to be independent of particular faiths is in the sense that they represent the overlapping concerns of a number of belief systems.

This view of what it means to be a professional religious educator raises important questions for the development of a philosophy for teacher training. Consider, for example, the following quotation from a course prospectus:

> The course seeks to place the teaching of religion firmly in an educational context by making no assumptions about, or preconditions for, the personal commitment of teachers, save to stress the role of the teacher in RE as that of educator. (Westhill College, nd, page 6)

This seems to be suggesting that the faith of the teacher is inherently irrelevant to professional work, in a sense that draws on the theory of the independent rationality of education. In contrast, I suggest it is essential that the religious commitment of the teacher is expressly addressed in teacher training. In particular, teachers should be encouraged to explore ways in which educational principles can be grounded in their own framework of beliefs. This is important in encouraging positive ownership of, and commitment to, the type of secular (in the first sense of the word) schooling appropriate to State schools. The aim will be to enable teachers with a variety of commitments to explore how their various frameworks overlap, and, thereby, provide a basis for a common approach to schooling. The exploration of the relationship between personal theology and educational principles should, therefore, be central to teacher education.

The Relationship Between Nurture and Education

I noted earlier that tension exists between the processes of nurture and schooling in the minds of some religious educationists (see page 24). Schooling is seen as being superior to the aspirations of a faith community to pass on its beliefs through nurture. In these circumstances, it becomes very difficult to consistently maintain that education and nurture are complementary, context-specific processes.

However, on the basis of the position I have been describing, genuine respect for the complementarity of the two processes can be maintained. Some of the conclusions that can be drawn from using this rationale are as follows.

First, it will be recognized that nurture is an essential foundation for schooling (Thiessen, 1987 and 1993). As thinking is not possible without the basic apparatus of a framework of beliefs, the fact that children come to school already embedded within such a framework is to be welcomed rather than regretted. Some of these frameworks will be religious, and some will not, but *all* provide a basis on which teachers can build. The experience that schooling offers will then develop, mature, and sometimes challenge this framework. However, it is quite unrealistic to regard it as a hindrance, to be done away with by an education that seeks to put children into some neutral, objective position, standing outside the influence of belief, and able to choose for themselves. To be self-determining, rational beings, all of us have to serve an apprenticeship as believers.

Second, nurture will be seen as the primary process, whereas schooling will be secondary. This is so because thinking cannot proceed outside of a framework of beliefs. Yet, these frameworks are matters on which people may reasonably differ. If we are to take the pluralist principle seriously, State schooling cannot prescribe *one* framework for *all* pupils. It has the much more restricted function of encouraging pupils, with a variety of frameworks, to develop strategies for functioning as citizens in the plural society in a way that both maintains the integrity of their fundamental beliefs *and* promotes community harmony.

Third, nurture promotes the rational holding of belief, even if it does not encourage children to be open-minded towards their beliefs in the way that liberals might wish. I have argued that holding a belief with absolute commitment and universal intent is rational. Furthermore, young children, particularly, are within their rights to believe, even though they may not have evidence for these beliefs. Parents and faith communities are justified in intervening in the belief-forming processes of their children as they have to be given some framework of beliefs if they are to think at all. Some people maintain that the alternative to this is to leave children free to make up their own minds. This is a nonsense. In fact, what happens when parents abdicate this responsibility is that children have their thinking formed by the implicit influences of the media and the peer group.

Nurture, however, must be distinguished from indoctrination. The debate as to *what* constitutes religious indoctrination is complicated and ongoing (see Thiessen, 1993). In terms of the framework developed here, it can be characterized as the exercising of one's right to believe while ignoring one's duty to do this responsibly. Indeed, part of a faith community's duty in nurture is to ensure that children face up to, and feel the force of, potential defeaters. This entails more than a trite and stereotypical survey of why all other beliefs are wrong. Instead, the purpose will be to encourage children to be self-determining, in the sense of taking responsibility for their own beliefs, and not simply living off the fat of someone else's faith. This can only happen by struggling with the challenges to faith. Furthermore, there is also an obligation on the faith community to encourage children to respect the right of others in society to believe differently. These responsibilities are heightened in the modern plural context of global communications, where there can be no excuse in terms of ignorance of alternatives, as is the case for more insular societies. Of course, decisions will have to be made as to the age at, and the degree to, which children are to be exposed to this struggle for mature faith. The decision will no doubt vary from child to child. In each case, there is a balance to be achieved between exposure and protection.

Both schooling and nurture, therefore, should support the exercising of rights and the fulfilment of duties. Nurture is not a threat to schooling if the approach to rationality of belief proposed here is accepted. The differences between them relate to differences in their context. Schooling is a State-sponsored activity, and so it is subject to the constraints of the pluralist principle. It has limited aims related to the responsibility it holds for promoting citizenship.

Nurture is not so constrained, so it can legitimately assume a faith. State-sponsored schooling should not theaten nurture if it takes account of its own limitations. Both processes should support the development of mature faith and, therefore, neither can legitimately support indoctrination. They are therefore, complementary, although, contextually, specific processes. Nurture within the Christian context, therefore, can appropriately be called Christian education without there being any contradiction in so doing.

❧ PART III ❧

—

Towards Evangelical Christian Foundations for Secular Education

---

CHAPTER EIGHT

Three Possible Approaches

Introduction

SO FAR, MY argument has been made in general terms, with a view to painting the broad outline of a secular approach to education that fulfils the pluralist principle of respect for diversity in matters of religion, where people may reasonably differ. These final chapters are intended to complement this by exploring how the Christian theological tradition with which I identify, conservative evangelicalism, might relate to this conception of education by providing its own distinctive rationale. The conservative Evangelical Christian tradition is a particularly useful case study since it is commonly perceived to be antagonistic to open religious education, and incapable of embracing religious difference or learning from others. Therefore, it represents a real test of the approach advocated here.

What is Evangelicalism?

Giving an exact definition of evangelicalism is an impossible task (Brown, 1981). Part of the reason for its being a contested concept is that it has undergone substantial changes over the years. However, this is not to say that certain fundamental, 'family' characteristics cannot be recognized.[1] Indeed, this *must* be so, otherwise the word would be devoid of meaning. In his substantial study of British evangelicalism, David Bebbington identifies four such characteristics:

> conversionism, the belief that lives need to be changed; activism, the expression of the Gospel in effort; biblicism, a particular regard for the Bible and what may be called crucicentrism, a stress on the sacrifice of Christ on the cross. Together they form a quadrilateral of priorities that is the basis of Evangelicalism. (1989, page 3)

Harold Netland puts it like this:

> Evangelicals hold certain things to be non-negotiable. While fully recognizing that God has revealed himself significantly through the created natural order and the moral conscience . . . Evangelicals maintain that God has revealed himself definitively in the Incarnation in Jesus . . . and that the Scriptures are the inspired, fully authoritative written revelation of God. All that is necessary for salvation and holy living is available in the special written revelation of God. No informed Evangelical would suggest that Christians have a monopoly on truth. Certainly there are elements of truth within other religious traditions and Evangelicals should always humbly recognize that there is always more that can be learned from those in other faiths. But Evangelicals emphatically maintain that God has revealed unambiguous truths about himself and about salvation in the Scriptures, truths that are absolutely unique and non-negotiable. Among these truths is, of course, the central Evangelical tenet that salvation is available only through the person and work of Jesus Christ and the accompanying corollary is that the good news of salvation in Christ must be proclaimed to all peoples in all cultures, regardless of their religious affiliation. (1991, page 294)

Of central importance is the attitude that Bebbington terms 'biblicism'. This is characterized by an insistence on the necessity of submission to biblical teaching, which is regarded as the authoritative source of insights into the nature of religious reality. It is this that provides the basis of both absolute commitment *and* universal intent for the Evangelical Christian. The thinking base of evangelicalism, therefore, is primarily defined in terms of a particular attitude to Scripture. Certain doctrines are uncontested as basic to Evangelical belief because they are considered central to the biblical revelation. An example is the deity of Christ. However, in principle, if it could be established successfully that this was *not* a biblical doctrine, then Evangelical consistency would demand its rejection. The same applies to the crucicentrism that Bebbington has identified.

In the final analysis, this biblicism rests on presuppositions based on the historical experience of many generations that God 'is a personal being, who communicated with our race in a directly personal way' (Hill, 1985e, page 5). Added to this is the belief that God safeguards the transmission of his message to future generations. Recognizing and accepting this is a product of conversion; it is not something that can be proved beyond doubt. Conversion goes hand-in-hand with experiencing salvation as it also entails personal acceptance of the benefits of Christ's death on the cross. These beliefs are expressed in a particular form of activism, evangelism, which is the attempt to gain acceptance of the truth of the Gospel by other people.

Three Approaches to Integration

Can a belief system like this embrace secular education as I have been describing it? To explore whether or not this is indeed possible, three approaches that Evangelical Christians might use to integrate their theology with an academic discipline like education will be reviewed. Here I am drawing on an essay by Ronald Nelson (1987). The first he calls the compatibilist approach. Its fundamental premiss is the autonomy of the discipline in question. This means that knowledge remains the same across cultures and religions. So, for example, there is no distinctively Christian or Islamic way of launching a space rocket. For theology to attempt to adjudicate on what *is*, or *is not* knowledge within another discipline is to move beyond the bounds of its legitimate role. To do this is sometimes described as making a *category*, or *type*, error. What this means is that it is a basic mistake to use language and concepts that are appropriate to answering theological issues in discussions of non-theological questions, such as those arising in education. I will call this the '*hand-over*' option, because theology 'hands over' authority to the discipline. Rational Christians are here expected to ensure that their beliefs are compatible with this autonomous knowledge.

The difficulties with this approach were discussed earlier (see Chapters 4 and 6). In particular, it takes no account of the need to set any discipline within a framework of beliefs that gives knowledge its significance and meaning (see pages 85–88). Claiming that a discipline is independent masks this, and usually means that presuppositions from a particular faith commitment are smuggled in under the cover of the claim that they deal with objective knowledge. This is very dangerous because these 'stowaway' presuppositions are controversial, but can easily be assumed to have the presumed independent authority of the discipline. Most of the stowaways in modern educational thought are either humanistic or from the tradition I have called radical Christian liberalism.

Nelson contrasts this with the *reconstructionalist* approach, which rejects the notion of the independent rationality or autonomy of any discipline from theology. As far as the reconstructionalist is concerned, *all* intellectual activity is based on theological presuppositions. We can call this the *take-over* option because Christian thought will seek to radically reconstruct a discipline on fully biblical foundations, and do away with all other interpretations. It will not compromise itself by seeking to find common ground with those 'outside of the truth'. It rejects any attempt to synthesize Christian and non-Christian thinking. I will leave detailed evaluation of this approach to the next section.

Nelson seeks to chart a way through this polarization by suggesting a third approach of 'transformation'. This recognizes the existence of shared assumptions and concerns between a discipline and religious belief, but maintains a distinctive role for theology. We can call this the *work-with* option, where Christian faith accepts some of the distinctive features of a discipline as givens, but develops them in a way that is integral to its own theology. Unlike compatibilists, *transformationalists* do not maintain that a discipline can have a rationality independent of religious belief. So, Nelson distinguishes between the common, *relative* horizon that scholars share as practitioners of a particular discipline, and the radically different *basic* horizons from which they may be operating (pages 336–7). This relative horizon, then, embodies the overlap of a number of belief systems. Its content will include the empirical findings of, and the concepts developed within, a discipline. However, decisions as to the ultimate *significance* and *purpose* of these elements of the common horizon, and judgements of truth, will be dependent on a person's *basic* horizon. For the religious person, this basic horizon will be theological.

A key concern for the Christian transformationalist is to do justice to the sovereign, and comprehensive claims of Christ.

The final goal, according to Nelson, is 'nothing short of the total translation of the discipline into its rightful place amongst the treasures of God's kingdom' (page 339). So:

> The transformationalist shares the reconstructionalist's vision of a wholesale reformulation into a fully Christ-honouring configuration but also recognises with the compatibilist that the discipline as constituted may have dimensions that commend themselves to integration with faith's assumptions and concerns.' (page 339)

This book is an attempt to develop a transformationalist approach to secular education. It seeks to define distinctive features for secular education that can be 'worked-with'—in other words, owned with integrity—by the majority of religious communities. I have done this by arguing that education, as a State-maintained enterprise, should not be treated as a discipline with an independent rationality, but, rather, must be seen as a process designed to achieve limited, although important, ends in a particular context. These are to do with helping children handle religious faith in the plural society in a way that is reasonable, responsible, and will enable those of different commitments to live together in harmony. In one sense, this is a radical redefinition of the concept of education. It entails defining the role of education and describing what it means to be rational in religion in ways that resonate with my Evangelical Christian beliefs. To this degree, I have adopted a reconstructionalist policy. In another sense, it is a return to the fundamental aspirations for secular education that are shared by many writers and are intrinsic to the pluralist principle. In this way, I have been faithful to the compatibilist aspirations of the transformationalist by appealing to arguments that are compelling for any professional educationist. The aim is to enable a Christian to develop a coherent theology of education, the outcomes of which are also acceptable to those of other religious positions.

This approach redefines the immediate challenge the believer has to meet in relating theology to secular education. The reconstructionalist develops a Christian view of education based on Christian first principles, stressing the antithesis with secular education. The transformationalist's task, however, is to decide whether or not a Christian can accept the constraints imposed by the fact that there are certain givens inherent in the secular, plural context. This means accepting that there are ethical limitations on the evangelistic goals Christians wish to pursue because education in common schools is an activity of the State. This is the case *even though* such goals would be quite legitimate in a different, perhaps more ideal, context. However, the ultimate goal of the Evangelical Christian will be to influence and transform the context so that these limitations will no longer exist. This strategy, therefore, moves beyond a compatibilist approach, which accepts secular education as the norm for all education.

Before moving to a detailed consideration of the transformationalist strategy, Nelson's analysis will be developed in more detail by reviewing influential Evangelical Christian exponents of the reconstructionalist and compatibilist approaches. The purpose of this will be to suggest, in more depth, why these two approaches are less than adequate.

Reconstructionalism Exemplified

Two influential exponents of the reconstructionalist strategy are Cornelius Van Til and Francis Schaeffer. Schaeffer was a student of Van Til's at Westminster Theological Seminary in Philadelphia, and became a highly successful popularizer of his thinking through the founding of the L'Abri community in Switzerland and publishing many books. They both see themselves as being within the Reformed tradition of Christian theology.

Discussion of knowledge in the Reformed tradition begins with the doctrine of God. According to Van Til, 'the Protestant doctrine of God stresses his self-sufficiency and therefore his ultimate control over all that comes to pass in the course of the history of the world' (1969, page 12). To deny this doctrine of the all-knowing God is to make an assault on his sovereignty, because it is to suggest that there is a principle of truth that lies *outside* God. Therefore, it is 'God's comprehensive interpretation of the facts that makes the facts what they are' (Van Til, 1980, page 7). Human knowledge can, then, only be true knowledge in so far as it corresponds to God's knowledge. Van Til puts it like this:

The only way for man to have any knowledge of either temporal or eternal things is for God to think for us in eternal categories and to reveal to us the measure of truth we can fathom. (1932, page 32)

The truly Christian mind, therefore, is not original in its thoughts, but, rather, is receptive to the *divine interpretation* of the facts (1932, page 64). Any confidence that our knowledge is true knowledge lies in our interpreting the world in terms of God's categories of thought.

This immediately raises the question of *how* human beings can know what God knows. For Van Til and Schaeffer, the answer is clear-cut: we know because God *communicates* to us. So, 'the idea of supernatural thought communication is inherent in the human situation' (Van Til, 1969, page 29). It is part of God's nature as Creator to do this and a manifestation of his complete control over history. God has chosen to achieve this through a written, propositional, and final revelation of himself in the pages of Scripture. The Bible, therefore, is an absolute authority presenting itself as 'God's communication of propositional truth, written in verbalized form, to those who are made in God's image' (Schaeffer, 1968a, page 89).

A further question arising from this view is how we can know that Scripture is, in fact, the revelation of the mind of God. In answering this, the writers in the Reformed tradition return to the nature of God. So, Van Til states that 'the arguments for Scripture as the infallible revelation of God is, to all intents and purposes, the same as the argument for the existence of God' (1980, page 68). As God is a self-sufficient being, and his knowledge cannot be judged by any principle outside of himself, then his revelation of this knowledge must also be self-sufficient. A self-explanatory God speaks with absolute authority (Van Til, 1969, page 15). Scripture, therefore, is self-authenticating, certifying its own validity. Furthermore, because it is in the nature of God to communicate himself and not to deceive, he will ensure the accurate transmission of the words of the original down the ages (Van Til, 1969, page 28, and Schaeffer, 1972, pages 90–4). An inerrant Scripture is presupposed from the nature of the God who is there.

Both Schaeffer and Van Til place great emphasis on the presuppositional nature of knowledge. For them, there are no such things as 'brute facts' as a fact can only be understood within some framework of presuppositions as this gives it its meaning (Van Til, 1976). For the Reformed tradition Christian, this framework is derived from Scripture. In sharp contrast, the rest of humanity derives its presuppositions from human reason. There is no neutral ground on the basis of which members of these two interpretative systems can enter into dialogue. One relies on the authority of God, and the other on the authority of human reason. According to these writers, a non-Christian can never know true facts (that is, facts as perceived by God) because, in their sin, they are rebelling against God (Perks, 1992, page 26). Sin, therefore, separates people from the only source of a true understanding of reality. Thus, it is seen to be nonsense to think that those who interpret a fact as dependent on God, and those who interpret it as *not* dependent on God have yet said something identical about this fact (Van Til, 1969, page 297). To argue for the neutrality of facts is to start with a presupposition that separates knowledge from the mind of God. So, there are two humanities:

> The one humanity says there is no God, or it makes gods in its own imagination, or it tries to come to God in its own way. The other humanity comes to the true God in God's way. There is no neutral ground. (Schaeffer, 1973, page 115)

The believer and the non-believer, therefore, have nothing in common (Van Til, 1969, page 295). Such a stark differentiation would seem to render real communication between the believer and non-believer impossible. However, Van Til is at pains to point out that this dualism exists in *principle* only (1969, page 22). In practice, it is impossible for non-believers to live completely by the logic of their position. God restrains them from doing this (1980, page 63). Rather, they find themselves living on what Van Til calls 'borrowed capital', derived from Christian presuppositions. These are principles of life that the rebellious person knows to be true deep down, and without which life would be meaningless. Such a person, therefore, is in ethical rebellion against that which is known but cannot be admitted to be the case. They know that the Christian foundation is the only rational foundation for any truth; there is no other tenable option. However, their heart rebels against this knowledge. It is only conversion through the work of the Holy Spirit that frees the individual from this internal conflict. It is this 'borrowed capital' that provides a basis for communication between Christian and non-Christian.

Both Schaeffer and Van Til are quite clear that there is no neutral ground that can provide a basis for a co-operative approach to education between Christians and non-Christians. The key principle in any contacts with non-Christian thought is that of *antithesis*. This is summed up simply in the statement that 'if anything was true, the opposite was false . . . Absolutes imply antithesis' (Schaeffer, 1968b, page 13). As far as Schaeffer and Van Til are concerned, it is this principle that is denied in modern thought in the cause of achieving harmony and good relations between those of fundamentally different persuasions. Their view is summarized well by Andrew Watts when he writes:

> The underlying principle of the book of Proverbs is: 'The fear of the Lord is the beginning of wisdom, and knowledge of the Holy One is understanding' (Chap. 9.10).
>
> If the finding of common ground were our aim we would be tempted to leave this principle to the end of the list, for it is one that will immediately separate Christian teachers from many energetic and talented people whose commitment to education is undoubted. But we know, that as far as our faith goes, this is where Christians must begin. It has often been said that when Christians let their faith be pushed to the end of the list the result has been an implicit acceptance of the secular humanist view that faith has no place in the search for knowledge nor in schooling. Thus our thoughts on schooling must begin with this principle. (1992, page 53)

So, the Christian approach to difference is not to look for common ground, but is 'loving confrontation' (Schaeffer, 1984). The deeply unsatisfactory nature of the non-Christian's present condition must be laid bare for them so that, like the prodigal son, the nagging memories of their true father are brought to the surface and repentance is thus stimulated. Direct confrontation with their current presuppositions is the only methodology that will demonstrate to children and adults their oppression by a false set of presuppositions. Only in this way can they be given a glimpse of the truth that they will find if they accept the authority of God's revelation.

For Van Til and Schaeffer, then, the most critical threat facing the Church lies in the temptation to abandon the principle of antithesis in favour of a synthesis with modern thinking, which leads inevitably to compromise and accommodation, as the line at which the final stand is taken is moved back in the cause of harmony and unity. For Stephen Perks, a leading exponent of this position in England, this is the fundamental problem with co-operating with schooling provided by the State. It is thoroughly infected by anti-Christian presuppositions (1992, pages 93 and 123).

Therefore, it would seem that there is little hope of integrating reconstructionalist thinking with the modern notion of a common system of education for all, which has as its goal the promotion of community harmony. Rather, the Christian involved in the educational process has either to work in Christian schools, ensuring that the pupils do not internalize the dualistic thinking of the modern world (Van Til described such schools as akin to Noah's Ark, symbols of separation and truth—1971, page 30) or work to establish a framework of Christian thinking within the common school that confronts the prevalent thinking of the age.

CRITIQUE

It is not my purpose here to provide a detailed assessment of this position. Its credentials as an Evangelical Christian theology are clear. However, I want to point to three difficulties of particular significance for our discussions.[3]

1: The Quest For Certainty

Both Schaeffer and Van Til are haunted by the need to be certain. The title of Stephen Perks' book *The Christian Philosophy of Education Explained*—note the 'the'—reflects this. There can be no acceptance of pluralism, no ambiguity, even within the Christian community. According to Schaeffer, modern man *has* to make a leap of faith, because he has no categories 'to enable him to be sure of the distinction between what is real and what is only in his head' (1972, page 61). In contrast, Christians have the certainty of true knowledge, because they hold the right presuppositions. Such confidence that one has direct access to the truth means that there is no recognition of any duty to learn from others. Furthermore, as those outside Christian truth are in such a position because of their ethical rebellion against what they *know* to be true, there can be no recognition of their rights to believe differently. There is no tenable belief outside of Christian belief. Religion is *not* a matter on which people may reasonably differ.

There are two fundamental problems with this approach. First, it is not clear why the presupposition of an all-knowing God should lead us to the conclusion that he must provide inerrant knowledge of himself. There seems to be no contradiction in the idea of such a God choosing *not* to reveal himself (or choosing only to do so partially). It is an arbitrary assertion that God cannot be regarded as self-sufficient if he does not make himself known absolutely to his creation.

Second, even if it could be established that an inerrant God necessitated an inerrant Scripture, this would still ignore the question of the accessibility of this Scripture to the human mind. Both Schaeffer and Van Til have assumed that the words on the page are perspicuous to the regenerate mind; they present themselves as brute fact because they are being read in the way that God reads them. Therefore, there can be no doubt or disagreement about what they mean. The possibility that we might read it wrongly does not seem to be countenanced. The disastrous effects of such ideas were clearly illustrated in Schaeffer's last book (1984), where he launches an attack on other Evangelicals who hold different opinions to him on such issues as patriotism, pacifism, feminism, and abortion. As far as he is concerned, there seems to be only *one* way of reading Scripture, and this reading is inerrant. The complicated issues of how we interpret and apply the Bible have been set aside in an attempt to escape the ambiguity that is part of any vibrant theology.

2: *The Possibility of Common Ground*

At the heart of this Reformed theological system is the idea that there are two absolutely distinct humanities: one gains true knowledge by employing the presupposition of the ultimacy of God's knowledge; the other propagates falsehood through its dependence on the ultimacy of human reason. There is no common ground, and no possibility of shared human knowledge. The possibilities of any secular middle ground, or a co-operative search for truth through encounter with belief systems other than our own, are rejected.

However, closer examination reveals that this rejection of any appeal to common ground is not rigorously pursued. Van Til wants to argue that, in the end, Christianity is the most reasonable position because it offers the only consistent, coherent explanation of human experience (Van Til, 1969, page 19; 1980, page 63). Reasoning with non-believers is not therefore in vain, because they can be led to see this. Schaeffer takes this tendency further, arguing that there are answers to the great metaphysical questions of life that can be rationally and logically considered, and communicated to others who inhabit a 'thought world' different to the Christian one (1972, page 19). Perks maintains that the intellectually honest non-Christian will not be able to deny the ultimate rationality of Christianity (1992, page 26). Therefore, it appears that argument by presupposition is not as isolated from some form of shared objectivity as the doctrine of two humanities asserts; there is *not* total apartheid.

These writers would contest this, denying that there *is* such a thing as objective evidence. They would import the notion of borrowed capital at this point, arguing that the non-Christian comes to see the truth of the Christian position because it is impossible to be consistent to non-Christian presuppositions. There are certain creation norms built into the structure of reality by God that, ultimately, cannot be escaped because of the work of the Holy Spirit in our lives, reminding us of their truth. However non-believers are in constant rebellion against these norms, in so far as they seek to be consistent to their own presuppositions.

The treatment of the idea of borrowed capital in this way, however, is perverse. Rather than see the idea of God implanting truths about himself in all people as part of his common grace or natural law, they have chosen to view it negatively, as evidence of God's condemnation of those who do not belong to his humanity. The very fact that it is 'borrowed' capital, emphasizes that it does not rightly belong to non-Christians as God's creation gift. Such arguments are adopted in order to protect the notion of a self-authenticating Scripture, which, in turn, rests on the notion of a self-sufficient God who only reveals himself, but cannot be discovered. I would suggest that such views are not truly Evangelical, because they ignore the doctrine of Creation in an overemphasis on the doctrine of the Fall.

My Irish colleague once pointed up the poverty of the notion of the two humanities by asking a simple question: 'Who would these theologians like to fly them to Dublin? A trained pilot who, they say, as a non-Christian has no real knowledge, or a Christian novice pilot in possession of true knowledge?'

3: An Issue Ignored

A final, and, from our point of view, important, shortcoming is that neither Van Til nor Schaeffer addresses the issue of the role of the State in relation to the transmission of religious belief through schools. They simply assume that teaching that was given to Israel, or the Christian community in the early Church, can be lifted and applied directly to the modern State. This does not take account of the enormous differences that exist between Israel as a theocracy, and modern understandings of the secular, plural, and democratic State. Neither does it admit the need to recontextualize the Gospel in new and changing political situations. Skillen (1990) has argued at length that this approach bypasses the crucial question of the legitimate role of government in relation to the transmission of religious belief.[4]

The result of ignoring this issue is the assumption that education, whoever provides it, should transmit 'the truth'. This is to make the mistake of allowing State education to give absolute definitions of the good life. It fails to recognize the difference between what can legitimately be pursued in education provided by the faith community, and the limited goals that can be pursued in the State context. The consequence is that the rights of citizenship of non-Christians are not fully acknowledged because Christians fail to recognize the controversial nature of their own beliefs in the public domain. Much more reflection on the question 'just how far will the Bible take us in providing direction for the differentiated political orders of the twentieth century, especially when most citizens do not acknowledge the Bible as a politically authoritative text?' (Skillen, 1990, page 24) is needed if totalitarianism and injustice are not to be propagated in the name of the Christian Gospel.

CHAPTER NINE

A Case Study in Relating Theology and Education

Transformationalist Aspirations

BRIAN HILL IS probably one of the most prolific, modern writers on Christian education.[1] He is Professor of Education at Murdoch University in Western Australia, and was, for many years, Editor of the Australian *Journal of Christian Education.* He is a self-confessed Evangelical. The themes of the authority of Scripture, the need for personal conversion in response to redemption made available through the death of Jesus Christ, and the importance of evangelism recur throughout his writings.

Of any Evangelical Christian writer seeking to reflect theologically on schooling, Hill probably comes closest to advocating the transformationalist stance taken in this book. However, I shall argue that, in the final analysis, his approach drifts into compatibilism. His work, therefore, provides a very interesting case study that will enable us to tease out the critical distinctions between these two approaches.

First, however, it is necessary to establish his transformationalist aspirations, which can be illustrated in three themes central to his work.

1: The Nature of Religious Belief

Hill's thinking on the nature of religious belief clearly demonstrates the main features of the position I have taken. One point that he has consistently argued over the years is that there is no neutral position in relation to education. A predominant concern in his work has been to make his readers aware of the presuppositions that underpin various educational theories. For the Christian, these will be drawn from Scripture.

Hill is however anxious to distance himself from the reconstructionalist notion that humanity is divided into just two types of person. Rather, he sees society as pluralistic, characterized by the presence of a variety of faith stances. He believes that the recognition of this fact should generate a state of mind in individuals that both recognizes 'the problematic status of all systems of belief and value', *and* accepts that all arguments for belief 'fall short of indisputable proof' (1985c, page 22). Therefore, a range of viable options for religious belief exist. One of the positive characteristics of such a state of mind is its tolerance towards other viewpoints, because it is realized that 'it is no longer possible to assume that every right-thinking person will be in agreement with oneself' (1985c, page 22). It is not, therefore, a moral failure to be a non-Christian; rather, pluralism of belief, and not consensus, is to be expected among people of intellectual integrity.

Although Hill's position is presuppositional and pluralist, he is not a relativist (1990b). So, for Hill, in one sense, *all* knowledge is *religious* knowledge because our ultimate beliefs, which are religious in character, provide the presuppositions for our knowledge. However, *true* knowledge is also accessible to all, irrespective of personal religious presuppositions, through an openness to evidence. This objectivity is grounded in the fact that all religions make claims about the nature of reality. Any non-realist theory of religious belief is, according to him, 'a lame-duck theoretical construct' (1990b, page 129). The reason for his passionate endorsement of realism is that he believes that no other explanation gives a basis for the strength of commitment that is characteristic of the religious way of life. So, he argues that:

> one cannot endorse a religion as imparting meaning, purpose and a sense of deliverance to one's life whilst at the same time believing it to be nothing more than a bracing myth-system. Religions are built on truth claims, and it is these which generate the trust and confidence which characterise the true believer. (1985b, page 4)

Therefore for Hill, it is quite justifiable that a religious belief is held with both absolute commitment *and* universal intent. Thus, it is to be expected that religious beliefs will create divisions between those who differ from each other (1988, pages 82–4) because conflicts of doctrine are disagreements about the nature of reality, which are of crucial importance.

2: The Nature of Society

For Hill, it is imperative that an adequate Christian analysis of education must engage with its current role in modern society. It is essential, therefore, to be clear on the nature of the context that it is serving. He argues that there are two features that must be embraced by any relevant theory.

First, it is secular. Hill agrees that Western society has a heritage rooted in Christian values, and that these used to provide the overarching religious canopy under which it operated. However, for a number of reasons, this situation has changed so that 'Christianity no longer provides the ideological canopy . . . our era is post-Christian' (1978b, page 12). Modern society is now plural, and, in order to ensure the harmonious existence of its citizens, Hill believes that public life must be secular. He is insistent that he is using this term in Newbigin's first sense of impartiality, not in its anti-religious sense (see page 114).

Second, Hill recognizes that the liberties of the secular and plural society are inherently unstable, and are in need of active protection. So, he agrees with Niebuhr that 'man's capacity for justice makes democracy possible: but his inclination to injustice makes democracy necessary' (1982, page 30). Therefore, 'the heart of values education in a school should be the endorsement of the idea of democracy' (1988, page 122). In Hill's view, this means that the school should teach commitment to a stance that embraces 'freedom to represent value systems and negotiate agreements within an atmosphere of respect for persons and tolerance of dissent' (1981, pages 167–8).

Of particular importance to Hill in his understanding of democracy is the notion of negotiation leading to consensus. Therefore, he 'pleads for conversations between ideological groups in our pluralist society that will bring forward positive agreements'. The purpose of these conversations will be to achieve 'some sort of democratic consensus on the common values and convictions that might impart some direction to secular education' (1971, pages 15 and 36). This process is essential if core values, which will hold a pluralist society together, are to be found.

3: The Role of Schooling

Hill sees the role of modern schools as providing 'that set of experiences which we desire formal education to provide for all children growing up in our society' (1971, page 29). However, he is insistent that this formalized institution of schooling is not the whole of education. Indeed, he regards it as one of the great failings of both the modern Church, and of educational theory, that the model of the compulsory school has come to be equated with the concept of education (1985a, Chapters 2 and 3). One symptom of this is the extent to which the school is now seen as responsible for solving all social problems. As far as Hill is concerned, 'we have put too many of our educational eggs in one basket' (1970, page 158).

Schooling, therefore, is limited in the function it can perform. 'The educational strategy of schooling is best adapted to enlightening students about the world, their culture and its options, increasing their capacity both for understanding and empathy' (1985a, page 56), to equipping them 'to cope with their technological and pluralistic environment' (1978b, page 8), and to 'helping them discover and enlarge their own particular interests and unique capacities' (1987a, page 71). Schooling also has an important function in promoting the ability to make relationships through community involvement (1982, Chapter 5). However, it is both wrong and impractical to expect schools to promote *particular* types of commitment when they are operating in the neutral middle ground of the secular, plural society. Therefore, he is a powerful advocate of other types of education that can fulfil this function, being, as far as I am aware, the only philosopher of education ever to have argued for the importance of voluntary Christian groups in schools (for example, 1987b).

COMPATIBILIST TENDENCIES

From this account it can be seen that Hill's position is very close to the transformationalist strategy I have been describing. Indeed, I am very happy to admit to being heavily influenced by his work. As we have seen, he rejects the reconstructionalism of those who want to capture schooling for Christ. However, he is also critical of the compatibilism of those who want to adopt radical Christian liberalism[2] as the cornerstone of educational theory, or even as the basis for a revision of Christian belief itself. He is looking for an authentically Evangelical Christian response, but one that allows Christians to be partners in the educational enterprise with those of other beliefs. Essentially, he wants to be in the secular educational world, but not of it to the degree that his beliefs and identity are defined by it.

However, in the final analysis, Hill loses his grip on his transformationalist aspirations, and slips back into a compatibilist mode that gives secular, educational ideas authority over his theological convictions. The net result is that he does not completely fulfil his ideal of thinking in a distinctively Christian way about education, and ends up compartmentalizing his mind into those areas controlled by Christian presuppositions and those not so controlled—something that he himself considers to be an unsatisfactory strategy (1982, pages 3–11). He thereby accepts a public/private distinction that accords a superior status to certain ideas, which have become influential in writings on secular education but which contradict his Christian beliefs. This can be illustrated by looking at three themes that Hill has developed in his writings over the years.

1: The Nature of Autonomy

The idea of autonomy is central to Hill's analysis of the spiritual nature of human beings (1990a, pages 44–6), representing as it does one of their 'most god-like attributes' (1983, page 41). The role of the educator is to maximize this authentically human characteristic. The antithesis of education is indoctrination, which 'seeks to pre-empt the right of individuals to make their own informed choices of values by concealing the existence of alternative views and discouraging critical evaluation' (1988, page 6), because it denies students their autonomy.

Hill regards education as an intentional activity to promote particular types of development in students. Therefore, it is a potential infringement of the individual's autonomy. If this autonomy is to be respected, the educator has the choice of either producing convincing, overriding reasons for intervening in the learner's life, or throwing in the towel and leaving learners free to learn, or not to learn, at their own discretion (1982, page 21). For Hill, intervention in the life of the child through education demands justification if it is to be an ethically acceptable activity.

Although Hill accepts that one starts with the right to freedom as the fundamental premiss, he does believe that there are good reasons for educators intervening and exercising power over their students. Indeed, intervention is inevitable if we take seriously the argument that all education is value-laden. He expresses this idea thus: 'if it is objected that one cannot be prescriptive about values and policies in a pluralistic society, then the result is not progressive education, but no education at all' (1982, page 34). However, very importantly, this is *not* a blank cheque for all and sundry to do what they like with children's minds.

Hill believes that the type of intervention characteristic of modern schooling is justified because it is built on values that are the result of a negotiated consensus, and have the sanctity of the individual at their heart. Teachers, therefore, are justified in interfering with the freedoms of children because these very freedoms cannot be protected without the active promotion of democratic values.

However, Hill's account of autonomy, and his views on intervention lead him into departing from his transformationalist strategy. Of particular importance is the lack of clarity as to exactly what he means by autonomy. Thus, in some places he seems to be sympathetic to interpreting it in terms of unfettered individual choice (1965b, page 140), so that 'education serves to widen choices and choice only exists where alternatives are perceived' (1974b, page 40). As we have seen, this emphasis on choice is characteristic of the view of religious belief that underpins the writings of many liberal educators, where the child is treated as an 'abstract, rootless chooser' (McLaughlin, 1992a, page 33). On this view is based the liberal belief that it is reprehensible to nurture children in a particular faith. I hasten to add that this is not Hill's view of nurture.

However, elsewhere, Hill's sympathies seem to be with a different understanding of autonomy, that interprets it in terms of self-awareness. Here, a key aim for education is that pupils should be in 'the state of the fullest possible awareness of the status of [their] beliefs' (1981, page 164). By this he means that students are enlightened concerning the ways they have come to hold their beliefs, the criticisms that could be made of them, their inevitable controversial status, and, finally, the fact of pluralism, and, therefore, an understanding of other, alternative beliefs. This seems to entail the importance of such things as examining evidence, weighing arguments, and recognizing the controversial status of ultimate commitments. Such a view will emphasize the importance of self-determination where 'the governing spiritual principle is that religious faith is something no one can have or exercise on behalf of others' (1965b, page 140).

However, self-determination and unfettered choice are not the same. The distinction between them can be illustrated by looking at an analogy that Hill uses (1990a, page 46), in which he notes that Jesus himself looked for an autonomous decision to follow him in potential disciples. Indeed, this is true, but, in order to achieve this, he did not insist that his hearers spend time examining a number of other options before following him. Neither did he refrain from seeking to influence them. Rather, in Jesus' ministry, autonomy meant that the potential disciple had realistically and honestly faced up to the challenge Jesus had presented and was prepared to freely submit to this. It meant personally 'owning' a belief in Jesus as Lord, rather than simply a desire to belong to the social group called 'disciples'. Such authentic commitment was not the result of a decision free from the influence of others, an unfettered choice. Neither did it require a knowledge of other alternative religious options such as offered by Confucius or the Buddha. Such knowledge may have been valuable for other reasons, but it was not a necessity for self-determination, and responsible commitment.[3]

Therefore, there is an important distinction to be made between self-determination and unfettered choice: the former emphasizes taking responsibility for the beliefs that shape us; the latter emphasizes individual freedom to choose. If Hill really *does* view autonomy as unfettered choice, then it certainly follows that *any* form of intervention in children's belief formation processes is wrong, or, at best, a necessary evil. However, if he sees it in terms of self-determination, then there is no reason for him to view intervention in this negative way. If he were to be consistent to his presuppositional view of knowledge, and his belief in the absolute truth of the Christian Gospel, then intervention is something that should be valued. It is both necessary for rational belief, and a valid expression of the universal intent with which the Gospel is held. It is actually non-intervention, not intervention, that needs justification in this case.

The fact that Hill himself both considers religious nurture, a very active form of intervention, to be important, and distinguishes it from indoctrination, shows that he should be able to accept the view of autonomy that I am proposing. That he continues to express unease with it, and to argue in places for a more individualist view, suggests a loss of confidence in his own transformationalist strategy, and a reversion to a compatibilist one, where a liberal interpretation of autonomy takes precedence over one drawn from his own Christian beliefs.

2: The Effects of Sin

The suspicion that he is allowing the liberal, individualistic view to colour his thinking is further illustrated by his treatment of the subject of sin. *As a Christian*, he argues that sin is the human characteristic that impairs our God-given capacity for self-determination (1973, page 266). Complete autonomy, therefore, is not available to non-Christians, who find that their freedom to choose is shackled by the human tendency to rebel against that which is known to be right.[4]

This fact of sin means that there is a problem to be faced. We cannot assume that children will be free to choose for themselves if we ignore this spiritual problem. Real choice can only come about as a result of an encounter with the Holy Spirit, who enlightens us, and restores our capacity for self-determination. 'By faith in Christ, the believer has restored to him an ever-widening area of free will' (1963, page 13). The logic of this belief is that true autonomy is only available through the Christian experience of redemption.

Hill recognizes that this insight poses a problem for teachers, for, 'if the good life is impossible without spiritual readjustment, then education must either include the objective of religious conversion or confine itself to a more limited objective' (1982, page 30). His response is to argue that redemption, in the explicitly Christian sense, *cannot* be pursued in secular education because it is a disputed belief in society. Schooling, therefore, must restrict itself to a more limited function. It can only bring the individual:

to the threshold of the substantive choices which really determine whether the learner will be a slave or free: hobbled by the caprice of his own warring soul, or liberated by a

resolve to seek first the Kingdom of God and His righteous-
ness. (1982, page 39)

It seems as though, in the final analysis, formal education cannot
deliver on this distinctively human capacity, the freedom to
choose, as it cannot legitimately offer, in the plural, secular
context, this redemption, without which autonomy is impossible.

The consequence of this argument, again, seems to be that
intervention, with a view to combatting the marring effects of sin
and initiating students into the experience of true freedom in
Christ, is justified *per se if* autonomy is an ultimate value. The
truth is that it is non-intervention, which leaves the child in the
grip of sin, that needs justification. In the context of State-
sponsored, secular schooling, this justification is provided by the
pluralist principle. It is, to put it bluntly, unethical to promote a
disputed belief like this, even though it is one believed to be
absolutely true and held with universal intent by Hill. This is a
restraint that has to be accepted if Christians are to contribute to
secular education, but it makes schooling less than the ideal and
nurture much closer to the ideal. These arguments are true to the
logic of Hill's transformationalist viewpoint. However, in his
writings, he appears to sympathize with that influential educational philosophy, which regards such intervention as unhealthy,
and adopts a view of 'rational' belief as unformed and unin-
fluenced by other people.

The danger is that, by privatizing the need for redemption,
Hill is endorsing a view that contradicts his own Christian
viewpoint. The logic of his Christian position is that, to teach
faith in Christ is to equip the child with an essential capacity for
true self-determination. Therefore, it is applicable to the public
domain. The acid test is whether or not Hill sees this bar on
teaching for religious commitment as a regrettable constraint
imposed by working in the secular, government-sponsored
context, but one that is not present in the faith community
context. If this is the case, then he remains true to his transformationalist position. If, however, he views teaching for
conversion as anti-educational *per se*, and the non-intervention-
ist strategy of secular education as the ideal in *all* contexts, then
he has slipped into the compatibilist mode. He is accepting the
superiority of values that are appropriate in the secular, public

domain over and against those that are distinctively Christian. It is this point that is the subject of my final criticism.

3: Education: Secular and Christian

The crux of Hill's argument lies in the distinction he makes between *education* and *schooling*. The latter is identified as being a formal process taking place in a compulsory, State-sponsored context. Those involved in schooling, therefore, are constrained, by virtue of their being State representatives, from transmitting beliefs and values that are inherently controversial. Schooling should not promote particular religious commitments.

However, for Hill, education seems to have much more comprehensive goals. Responsibility for it extends beyond professional schoolers to, for example, parents and church members. Their work is not as restricted as the professionals' because the pupils or their parents have chosen to participate in such activities. Furthermore, the limitations of having to operate in the neutral middle ground of the secular state no longer apply. It would seem, therefore, that educators working in these 'non-schooling' contexts should be free to transmit certain beliefs and values in a way that schoolers are not, as long as this is not carried out in an indoctrinatory fashion. The negotiated consensus of the school in the State system is, perforce, secular. In contrast, the consensus the 'educator' works to can be that of a particular religion, as the demands of the pluralist principle disappear in the context of the family, church, or voluntary organization. It would seem, therefore, that education in these contexts is free to promote the particular value commitments of that community or family as all education, according to Hill, promotes commitments. As a Christian we would expect him to applaud such teaching as the means whereby children are offered liberation from the shackles of sin.

When, however, we examine Hill's views on Christian education, nurture, and evangelism, it seems that he is unclear on this point. In the final analysis he seems to feel that schooling is the model to which all other forms of education should be compatible. A comprehensive treatment of this question appears in *The Greening of Christian Education*. In this book, he states that Christians 'are free to build their educational theories on more comprehensive views of the world derived from Christian beliefs' than are those who operate in the public, secular domain. However, he also says that 'they must then show that what they are doing deserves the title education', which has now 'become attached to one of the processes of socialisation in a multi-faith society and is regarded as referring to the [relatively] neutral business of expanding human awareness and capacities rather than fixing certain beliefs and behaviours in the captive learner' (page 68). On this basis, he then goes on to argue that the concept of Christian education is incoherent because one cannot, without there being internal contradiction, both teach for Christian commitment *and* educate. However, in maintaining this, Hill has here equated education with what we earlier identified as the more limited process of schooling. The whole of the education enterprise has been subordinated to the aims of schooling.

Even so, Hill still wishes to give a role to the teaching ministry of the Christian community, the function of which is 'to aim by enlightenment to trigger commitment to God in worship and the neighbour in mission' (1985a, page 71). However, he does not wish to call this education, seeing it, instead, as evangelism, if it is assumed the audience is non-Christian, or nurture, if it is assumed the audience is Christian (1990a, pages 146–7). Again, it seems that the distinctions between education and schooling that we discussed previously disappear, and that the modern concept of education is now identified with, or at least must operate on the same basis as, the process of schooling. The initial smaller, more limited concept has consumed the larger, so that the Christian transformationalist vision has become limited to one that is compatible with a secular rationale. Hill's reluctance to allow the processes of nurture and evangelism to be classed as educational activities, suggests an accommodation to the notion that public-domain activities are superior to private-domain ones, rather than a simple concern to correct the terminology.[5] Such activities do not seem to 'deserve' (1985a, page 68) the title education.

To conclude, Hill places a high value on faith groups co-operating in the educational enterprise. He writes:

the only viable policy for a multifaith society is to encourage mutual respect for persons, constructive social interaction in the middle ground of the secular society and dialogue as between friends about their basic religious differences. (1988, page 42)

In order to achieve this, schooling in the compulsory context has to be limited in its goals; it depends on a degree of consensus, and the acceptance of a restricted role for government schools. Therefore, it cannot promote particular commitments. This far many Evangelicals would go.

However, there is a world of difference between this negotiated, pragmatic consensus being *necessary* in the secular democracy of a plural society, and the same principles being the *ideal model* for *all* education, including that within the Church. From being simply a necessary compromise to ensure justice, a model of education appropriate to a plural democracy has become an ideal in its own right, with a rationality independent of religious commitments. The Christian needs to have good reason to refrain from proclaiming the message of redemption through Christ; the ethical constraints imposed by schooling in the secular democracy provide such reasons. However, these constraints disappear in the context of the faith community, but Hill seems to draw back from this latter conclusion. He argues that the Christians of the early Church sent their children, in good faith, to pagan schools. However, it is very unlikely that they applied the principles of that pagan education to the education of their children in the contexts of home *and* Church. It is this that Hill seems, on occasions, to be suggesting should happen now.

THE NEED FOR DISTINCTIONS

Hill's loss of confidence in his transformationalist strategy, I suggest, is related to the fact that, at certain crucial points, he fails to make important distinctions. Four of these merit particular comment.

First, he has conflated the notions of self-determination and individualism. His presuppositional view of knowledge should lead him on to accepting that it is an inevitable part of the human condition that our believing is shaped by others. None of us are free-floating individuals; all of us are products of our upbringing. To be self-determining is to appreciate the fact that we are so shaped, to be aware of alternative sources of shaping, and to determine for ourselves, as we gain in maturity, those beliefs that will mould our lives in the light of the critical reflection that marks us out as rational beings. To be self-determining is to be a responsible believer.

In individualism, however, there is an antagonism to shaping by others, and an embracing of what we might call radical freedom, or unfettered choice. This thinking must question the activities of nurture and evangelism, and can only accept a transmission model of education in areas where there is no dispute as to the objective status of its content. Individualism reflects the values of Western liberalism, whereas self-determination reflects those of a framework that respects both the integrity of the individual and our relatedness as members of particular communities. Furthermore, it takes seriously the presuppositional nature of knowledge, which individualists find sits uneasily with their position. Those who support individualism also find themselves offended by the inherently interventionist nature of education. Those who promote self-determination are, however, happy to accept their responsibility to intervene, as long as it is exercised in a non-indoctrinatory fashion.

Following on from this is the second point, which is that, on occasions, Hill seems to equate the notion of indoctrination with the planned transmission of beliefs. So, he states that 'if one is teaching for Christian commitment in the context of compulsory classroom instruction, then indoctrination . . . is occurring' (1985a, page 69). Elsewhere, he accepts an understanding of indoctrination as the passing on of beliefs in a way that hides their problematic status and presents them as unchallengeable facts seeking merely to achieve conformity (1990a, page 72–6). This view should not exclude education that aims to create Christian commitment in Church and home contexts, if proper attention is given to respecting students' rights to believe differently, and if they are encouraged to fulfil their duties in relation to the beliefs they hold. However, as we have seen, Hill appears uneasy about *any* form of formal education that seeks to achieve such commitment, presumably because it precludes choice. However, this is to return to the point regarding the problem of confusing self-determination with individualism.

Third, he seems to feel that the constraints that rightly apply in State-sponsored schooling must also apply in any formal learning environment. So, he writes that 'schools for today's society, whatever their sponsors, must have purposes which are secularly defined' (1971, page 13). His concern is that such contexts are compulsory, and that to teach with the aim of creating commitment is wrong in such circumstances. However, the constraints on secular schooling are to do with the fact that they are an activity of the State, *not* because they are compulsory. These constraints, therefore, do not apply to other contexts where there is no such State control. His objection to transmitting beliefs, or teaching for commitment in all compulsory, formal educational contexts is again linked to his lingering attachment to the ideal of individualism, and its abhorrence of intervention in the belief-forming process. Therefore, he seems unhappy with parents placing their children in formal educational contexts that are built on the values of a particular faith tradition.

It is this attachment to individualism that underpins his opposition to Christian schools,[6] and his unease with the concept of Christian education. The logic of his transformationalist position, then, is that teaching for commitment should be acceptable within faith communities, where it is quite legitimate to assume a value system. Certainly, I share Hill's concern that the Church might be tempted to invest all its educational energies in the model of formal schooling. Neither, like Hill, do I endorse indoctrination in the context of the Christian community. However, I certainly do *not* accept, as Hill seems to, that this means that the *only* legitimate kind of formal education is that appropriate to secular classrooms.

Finally, it is important to clarify further the use of the terms *secular*, *public*, and *private*. The view of the secular that Hill supports is that of a middle ground where there is no one, overarching belief canopy derived from any of the major, but disputed, systems of belief. Such a context can be described as public in the sense that it is a realm where all people can participate, whatever their particular religious commitments. A religion can, then, legitimately be described as private in the sense that it cannot be treated as providing the framework for this State-sponsored, secular domain. Religious beliefs are, however, still public in the much more fundamental sense that they are held, quite legitimately, with universal intent and that adherents will view their beliefs as applying to all people. They will, therefore, seek to persuade others. All this is acceptable to the transformationalist position I have been outlining. However, it cannot accommodate the view that secular values are public in the sense of being superior to religious values, a position that is akin to secularism. Here, religious belief is made private in a much more fundamental sense.

Just occasionally, it appears that Hill sees religious belief as being private in this more radical sense in arguing that Christian education must be defined by secular criteria. In this case, 'public' values have a universal applicability that 'private' religious beliefs do not. The standards applicable to secular or public activities are treated as the ideal. So, the secular model of education is treated as the only acceptable one. However, this position represents a drift from an understanding of the secular as an impartial, middle ground to the idea that secular values are the only values that can be legitimately treated as universal. This is the essence of compatibilism. Its outcome is to set the secular and the religious in opposition to each other, a position that Hill is actually very concerned to avoid.

❈ CHAPTER TEN ❈

A Return to the
Transformationalist Strategy

Introduction

BRIAN HILL HAS made a significant contribution to the development of an Evangelical Christian, transformationalist strategy for education. His main difficulty in making a complete success of this venture is that, on a few occasions, he interprets secular educational values in a way that gives too much house room to radical Christian liberalism. He thereby falls into the compatibilist trap of handing over absolute authority to secular education, to which faith is expected to bow. He does this because he is concerned to avoid the learning sickness that leads some religious people to think, mistakenly, that indoctrination and transmitting tribal attitudes are sound educational goals (see Chapter 1). I wish to suggest, however, some modifications to Hill's position that maintain the integrity of Evangelical Christian faith, but still avoid promoting learning sickness without thereby becoming compatibilist.

To avoid compatibilism, we need to change the question we ask. The *unhelpful* question is 'how can we integrate our beliefs with the *independent* discipline of education?', because this treats education as an ultimate given, a sort of sacred monolith. Instead, we need to recognize that secular education serves a particular context, and this has its own distinctive characteristics. The question then becomes whether or not our Christian beliefs can be applied within secular education in a way that honours both the needs of the context *and* our beliefs. So, we need to ask whether or not Evangelical Christians can maintain their religious integrity if they use the 'work-with' approach that I have described as being necessary in the secular educational context. The theological jargon for this is to ask whether or not Christian theology can *contextualize* with modern, secular education.

Evangelicals and Contextualization

The key premiss for Evangelicals who accept the importance of contextualization is that the fundamental core of beliefs basic to Christianity can be expressed in different ways in different cultural contexts. This core represents the most important truth claims as to the nature of reality. Because they can be expressed in different ways, there are, therefore, a number of different authentic forms of Evangelical Christianity. The danger that concerns Evangelicals is that this attempt to contextualize opens up the way for compromise and the inconsistent reconciliation of differing schools of thought (syncretism). The risk is that in using a 'working-with' approach to a culture, our Christianity is 'taken over' (see pages 109–10) by this culture, and its fundamental truth claims are violated in the process. How, then, is the line to be drawn between effective contextualization and compromise?

Bruce Nicholls attempts to answer this question by distinguishing between what he calls the *prophetic principle* and the *accommodating syncretistic principle* (1980, pages 59–62). Applying these results in two different approaches to contextualization (Hesselgrave and Rommen, 1989, pages 51–9). The prophetic approach sees the Gospel as a body of God-revealed content that has to be translated into different cultural forms in order to speak to these cultures. The application of this principle means that the Gospel is always reforming. So, although, in the first instance, the characteristics of a particular societal context are accepted, the Christian will, ultimately, seek to *change* this context, in so far as Christian norms are not being fulfilled. For Nicholls, this principle is characteristic of successful contextualization. The accommodating syncretistic principle, on the other hand, emphasizes the *relativity* of the message, and demands that a faith position compromises its own integrity in an encounter with a new context. The prophetic principle, then, supports the validity of a *culturally expressed* message, whereas the accommodating syncretistic principle will accept nothing short of a *culturally determined* theology.

The accommodating syncretistic approach is a way of doing theology that interprets biblical texts solely in response to the demands of the context. The call made by John Hick and others[1] for Christians to abandon their traditional belief in the uniqueness of Christ is an example of this. Essentially, it is a compatibilist strategy because theology 'hands-over' the task of defining truth to criteria drawn from within the context. So, in the case of John Hick, the need for dialogue in the modern multifaith world is seen to rule out belief in the uniqueness of Christ. It does not then matter what the text of the Bible, or the tradition of the Church might have to say; if the modern context demands that we move beyond this belief, then this is what we must do. The unchanging anchor is the demand made by the context. However, for the prophetic principle, the anchor is the essence of the Gospel message, understood in a way that is responsive, and relevant to a number of different contexts.

Of course, this analysis raises the question of whether or not it is possible to identify a 'culture-free' essence to the Gospel. Most Evangelical scholars now recognize that 'the Gospel' is *always* an interpreted message. At the same time, they also insist that the biblical text itself places limits on its own interpretation. The meanings that can be attributed to it are not so indeterminate that we do not find considerable agreement. Chris Wright, Editor of the Evangelical theological journal *Themelios*, unpacks this idea when he argues that the Old Testament provides us with a paradigm, in the sense of being a concrete exemplar of God's action, but that it does not offer, in Israel, a normative culture. He writes:

> The Old Testament thus provides us with both the matrix of belief and understanding which corresponds to reality (i.e. that governs and shapes our world view) and it shows us a historical exemplar of what that means in practice for one human community—both through its achievements and in its self-conscious and self-critical failures. (1991, page 46)

Here, Wright is affirming a principle that is fundamental to the Evangelical tradition, namely that there are timeless truths that have been expressed *within* the historical process, but are not *confined* to it. Just as many different maps can accurately express the same reality depending on their function and perspective, so different interpretations and applications can reflect the timeless Gospel accurately. However, a map can never legitimately represent reality differently from the actuality; there are limits on the cartographer's interpretation. So, too, with the theologian and the Gospel.

René Padilla describes an Evangelical approach to contextual-ization as follows:

> The challenge . . . is to transpose the message from its original historical context into the context of present-day readers so as to produce the same kind of impact on their lives as it did on the original hearers or readers. (1980, page 65)

Charles Kraft, has expressed this in terms of what he calls the *dynamic equivalence model*, which he defines as being:

> A kind of 'translation' of the meanings of the church from the cultural forms of the source to the cultural forms of the receiving culture that function in such a way that they convey equivalent meanings. Only by changing the forms can the meanings be preserved. (1980, page 219)

Effective contextualization is not simply to transpose a set of biblical words to a new cultural form, but, rather, is to commu-nicate equivalent meanings in a form that *makes sense* for any particular culture. This is no easy task. The task is the trans-culturation (not simply the translation) of the message with the aim of representing 'these historical events as if they were clothed in contemporary events' (Hesselgrave and Rommen, 1989, page 65).

There is, I suggest, agreement among Evangelicals that the timeless and identifiable Gospel message is *normative* in the contextualization process. The crucial point is that, in an encounter with culture, Evangelical writers agree on the prin-ciple that the Gospel is performing an adjudicating function by, ultimately, standing in judgement on the culture, and, thereby, setting limits to the process of contextualization. It can never be restricted to an illuminating function, simply providing spiritual glosses for cultural norms. In the final analysis, it is the Gospel that is normative, although adjustment can take place in order that the message can be applied within another culture. In commenting on the World Council of Churches General Assembly in 1991, Nicholls said that:

> This issue of defining the boundaries between faithful contex-tualization and destructive syncretism is fundamentally a hermeneutical one of rightly exegeting [expounding] Scrip-

ture and interpreting it in the context of different cultures. (1991, page 5)

Evangelicals are still in the early stages of discovering what this process entails. However, one thing is clear. Theology that either seeks to work exclusively from 'above to below' (the take-over, reconstructionalist option), or exclusively from 'below to above' (the hand-over, compatibilist option), will be inadequate. A balance of *both* these approaches has to be maintained. In the past, Evangelicals have not always achieved such a balance. In a provocative pamphlet on responding to religious pluralism, Colin Chapman expresses the point as follows:

If I were to go about it in the way that I (and probably many of you) were trained, I would have to begin with revelation and study biblical passages relating to the uniqueness of Christ. I would then try to fit this teaching into some kind of systematic theology; and the final stage would be to discuss the practical applications of the biblical and theological truths. (1992, pages 5–6)

This is theology from above. Chapman maintains that this needs to be balanced with an approach that starts with questions of practical application. His argument is that you cannot read Scripture properly if you have not asked the right questions of it in the first place. Those using the 'theology from above' approach assume that the questions are defined by the text. However, the Bible is a dynamic book and, through it, God speaks to situations never envisaged by the biblical writers. In order to meet the challenges of the modern world, theologians have to discern what the relevant questions are and ask these in their study of Scripture. These are found by means of a study of the context. To do this, is to enter the hermeneutical circle (or 'spiral' as he calls it) between context and theology at a different point to that at which it is usually entered. Chapman's point is that some important questions which would otherwise be ignored are thereby given their proper attention.

Increasingly, Evangelical writers (for example, Kirk, 1990; Sugden, 1990; Stott and Coote, 1980; Storkey, 1991) are emphasizing the need for theologians to take account of the fact that their 'Sitz-im-Leben' (situation-in-life) shapes their thinking, and influences the questions they ask of Scripture. In education, the failure to do this has meant that Evangelicals have confined themselves to considering the educational needs of children as defined within the Sitz-im-Leben of the church community. This emphasizes the evangelistic and nurture aspirations of this community, legitimate in their place, at the expense of ignoring the Sitz-im-Leben of the secular context. Here, the education offered has to be appropriate for all children in a State-controlled process. The secular context poses some very different questions. If account is not taken of them, the danger is that Evangelicals simply pursue their own interests at the expense of other people.

Evangelical Contextualization and the Process of Education

This book has been an exercise in just the sort of process Chapman recommends. I have sought to tease out the questions that are raised by the attempt to include religion in the process of secular education. Christian theology should be encouraged to respond to these, and, where possible, to baptize secular educational insights by incorporating them within its own frame-work. By this is meant that secular insights are used in a Christian way, and supported by a Christian rationale. Educa-tion, then, is acting as a midwife to the process of theological reflection.

The key questions that have been identified are as follows.

1.   Can Evangelical theology accept the view of religious belief described in Chapter 6?
2.   Can Evangelical theology be open to other religions in being able to both learn from them, and work alongside them in the educational task of preparing young people for life as citizens in the religiously plural society?
3.   Can Evangelical theology accept that State-provided educa-tion has a limited function in relation to religion? Furthermore, can it endorse the pluralist principle and accept its own disputed status in the public realm?

These questions pick out the distinctive elements of secular education as I have described it. If Evangelicals are to adopt a transformationalist policy towards it, these are the principles that they must be prepared to 'work-with'. If they *cannot* be affirmed, then the only option left is the reconstructionalist one.

In response to the first question, I would simply wish to point out that many of the writers whose ideas have been drawn on in describing rational belief in the preceding pages are themselves Evangelicals.[2] Furthermore, the final report from the Anglican Evangelical Assembly in 1992, which tackled the issue of pluralism, resonates with the themes that form the framework of Chapter 6. Certainly many Evangelicals would identify with the work of Lesslie Newbigin,[3] who has built his ideas on the writings of Michael Polanyi.

Perhaps more critical than this is to establish that a religion which claims to have access to the truth can be open to change and the possibility of learning from others. Of fundamental importance here is the distinction that many Evangelicals make between their *own* understanding of the authoritative text of Scripture and the *true* meaning. Hermeneutics (the study of biblical interpretation) teaches us that we all read the text from our own cultural perspectives, which can blind and imprison us. This has made Evangelicals aware of the need to listen to others in their quest to unearth the meaning of Scripture. As John Goldingay, principal of St John's College, Nottingham, puts it:

> The fact that we read with the advantages and disadvantages of our background and commitments is reason for doing so reflectively and self-critically rather than unthinkingly, if we want to have a chance of seeing what is actually there in the text. (1993, page 7)

Further on in the article, he also notes that the same text may have a diversity of legitimate applications. So, to pick up Chris Wright's ideas, there is a continuing task to fulfil in reapplying the paradigm in new situations. In a very real sense, therefore, theology is a creative activity. Such an attitude is in stark contrast to that of the reconstructionalists, as we saw earlier. However, it does not lose its grip on the authority and objectivity of the text. Although this is only the briefest overview, it is enough to indicate that many Evangelicals are quite able, with complete integrity, to accept the view of rational religious belief I have proposed. They would not, however, be able to accept the view that I discussed in Part I of the book.

This, then, leads us to the second question, regarding the attitude of Evangelical theology to other religions. Evangelicals are usually associated with hard-line exclusivism which regards other religions as false. However, there is, among Evangelical writers, an increasing acceptance of the fact that God can speak through, and be present in, other religions, and that Christians can learn from members of other religions. In his book *Christianity and Other Religions* (1984), Norman Anderson argues for the Evangelical belief in the uniqueness of Christianity, laying out a case for the mutual incompatibility of the world's religions. At the same time, he points out that there is a universalist tinge in Scripture that Evangelicals have often ignored. So, he argues that there is truth in other religions, because God has not left himself wholly without witness within them. When non-Christians are converted to Christianity, Anderson observes that, although there is a discontinuity between their previous beliefs and their new way of life, 'there is so often the strong conviction afterwards that it was the living and true God who was dealing with them in the days of their pre-Christian wrestlings' (pages 173–4).

Nigel Biggar develops this, noting that people do come to faith in Christ via another religion (1989). So, Abraham received the call of God as a pagan (page 32). Similarly, Anderson claims to know of more than one Muslim whose study of the Qur'an made them seek Christ (1984, page 173). Christopher Lamb makes a parallel point when he argues that, if there were no truth at all in other religions, it would be impossible to even begin communicating Christian ideas to their adherents (1989, page 22). Christopher Wright, too, puts forward a similar argument in an important editorial in *Themelios* (1993). It seems, then, that Evangelicals are not averse to accepting that true knowledge of God is to be found in other religions.

Biggar also argues that Christians have things to learn from non-Christian religions, and cites the case of Abraham receiving the blessing of Melchizedek (1989, page 32). Christians have borrowed ideas from those around them and incorporated them into their own thinking—indeed, they have to if they are not to live a totally isolated existence. Learning from others can enable the Christian believer to become a *better* Christian, as new ideas are incorporated into the Christian framework. Any honest assessment of the development of Christian theology *must* recognize how it has drawn from the experiences of encounters with other faiths (Biggar, 1989, page 31). Truth is to be discovered by being 'out there' as well as 'in here'. To accept this is to affirm the notion of one truth for all of God's created beings, and to deny the relativism implicit in the acceptance of the notion of community-bound truth. To be a spiritually mature Evangelical Christian, entails not being frightened of encountering truth outside the Christian community. On the contrary, it means being prepared to engage with the non-Evangelical world as a learning experience, promoting spiritual growth. For example, the experiences of the children of missionaries shows how cross-cultural encounter enables them to fulfil the responsibility for their own belief formation in a more comprehensive way than is the case with children confined to a monocultural experience.[4]

The theological rationale for the position that I have been putting forward is usually expressed in terms of 'natural law', 'common grace', or 'the way of wisdom' (for example, Martin, 1989; Barclay, 1984, Chapter 5). Lying behind these is the notion that God has instituted certain standards in the world in such a way that they are part of the nature of things, and accessible to all people. Norman Anderson cannot agree with Raymond Panikkar that the Hindu is saved by Christ by means of his Hinduism (1984, pages 172–3) because he wants to hold on to the uniqueness of Christ's incarnation. He can, however, accept that a Hindu finds 'Christ' in the nature of things as created by God. Albert Wolters expresses this idea as follows:

> As human beings, we are so interwoven into the fabric of a norm-based creation that in spite of our religious mutiny we conform to creational standards 'by nature' by virtue of our very constitution as creatures. (Wolters, 1985, page 25)

The fact that true knowledge is built into the structure of creation explains, from the Christian perspective, why there is so much overlap between the different belief systems. This means that Christians can learn from non-Christians and share common concerns with them. Real partnership, therefore, is possible.

Now, for the third question. Can Evangelicals endorse the pluralist principle and a view of secular education that sees the promotion of a harmonious community life in the religiously plural society as its chief *goal*? First, we should note that, among Evangelicals, there is increasing acceptance that incarnating the kingdom of God cannot be achieved in isolation from an attempt to address the issues that face all of humanity in the modern world (for example, Stott, 1984). Evangelicals generally recognize that there is more to a life of mission than just evangelism.[5] It would be a self-contradictory Christianity that did not feel *some* responsibility for the well-being of society as a whole.

Second, there is an increasing recognition of the importance of orthopraxis, alongside the traditional Evangelical emphasis on orthodoxy (Kirk, 1990). Nigel Biggar has pointed out that it is important that Christians bear witness to the Gospel 'evangelically' (1989). By this he means that the methods used, and the attitudes held towards the non-believer must be appropriate to the nature of both the Gospel and the Christian God. For example, as people saved by grace, Christians cannot assume those who do not believe are more perverse than themselves (page 29). His conclusion is:

> that the manner and means by which the Christian confession may be made are subject to restriction by the moral implications of that confession; and that these moral restrictions become tighter in the case of public service. (page 37)

The Christian teacher, wishing to bear witness to the Gospel evangelically, cannot escape the responsibility to do this in a way that respects the rights of fellow citizens. It is simply a contradiction in terms to regard coercion, or political imposition as Evangelical ways of spreading the Gospel. Yet, it is amazing how often protecting the power base of Christians is confused with sharing the good news.

Others have pointed out that the concept of justice is inextricably linked to the belief that God created one humanity (for example, Hobbs, 1987; Cook, 1978). Rights of citizenship are not determined by a person's religion, nor are they lost by failure to belong to the community of God's redeemed, but are rooted in membership of God's one created humanity (Skillen, 1990, page 198).

Certainly, it would seem hard to describe a position as consistently Christian if it denied basic rights of citizenship to others purely on the grounds of their religious faith, yet this is exactly what was proposed in an influential pamphlet published in 1988 by two Christian teachers.[6] In it, they recommended that Parliament pass legislation so that Committee A of Standing Advisory Councils for RE (SACRE) and of Agreed Syllabus Conferences (ASC) should 'revert to that envisaged by the 1944 Act—it should be made up of members of Christian denominations other than the Church of England' (page 29).

This needs a little explanation. SACREs are local bodies that Local Education Authorities (LEAs) in England and Wales are required to set up to monitor and advise on the delivery of religious education. An ASC is created to draw up the LEA syllabus. Once adopted, the syllabus is legally binding on most schools maintained by the LEA. Committee A of these two bodies is constructed to reflect the religious composition of the locality served by LEA. The purpose of having this committee is to achieve agreement between the various religious communities on the nature of religious education in its schools.

It is true that, in 1944, the intention of the Act was that this committee should consist of representatives from Christian denominations other than the Church of England (the Anglicans had representation on another committee of their own). The reason for this was that the important religious pluralism in society in 1944 was that within the Christian Church. However, English society has changed since then. In most LEAs, there are now significant non-Christian minority communities. During the 1970s and 1980s, these communities were offered places on Committee A, although the wording of the law had not changed. The purpose of doing this, was to give them a voice in debates about the sort of religious education that was to take place in the schools to which they sent their children, and for which they paid through their local taxes. The effect of the clause proposed by the two Christian teachers would have been to *remove* all these non-Christians from Committee A. Thus, they would be denied the opportunity to influence the religious education provided by local government. One shudders at the thought that such disenfranchisement would be carried out in the name of the Christian Gospel, and the effect that this would have had on community relations in cities like Birmingham does not bear thinking about. Fortunately, this suggestion never reached the statute book.

The crucial point is that a concern to develop a common vision for the common good is surely a theological necessity for any consistent Gospel Christian. In matters of public policy, Christians should feel a responsibility to look after the interests of people from other faith communities, and not just those of Christians, or even more narrowly, Christians who share their theology. Os Guinness has made a particular case for this, maintaining that Evangelical Christians should affirm the importance of religious liberty in their philosophy of the public place (1989, 1991). He argues that it is a matter of urgency that Christians address the question of how, in a world of increasing pluralism, people are to live and work alongside those they differ from at the deepest levels. He proposes the notion of 'chartered pluralism' as the way forward. Guinness describes his approach as follows:

> a vision of religious liberty in public life that, across the deep religious differences of a pluralistic society, guarantees and sustains religious liberty for all by forging a substantive agreement, or freely chosen compact, over three things which are the '3Rs' of religious liberty: rights, responsibilities and respect. (1991, page 43)

Guinness accepts that these are principles for peace rather than articles of faith (1991, page 47) in the sense that the different 'signatories' to such ideals will ground them in very different theological frameworks. The present state of intellectual divisions in modern pluralistic societies simply does not permit agreement at the level of fundamental beliefs. However, significant, though limited, agreement is still possible at the level of outworking of beliefs. These agreements can happen where there is an overlap of a number of belief systems, and this occurs in such a way that consensus can be achieved on how fundamental differences are to be handled in the public arena so as to generate a common vision for the common good. For the Christian, this vision is rooted in a kingdom ethic that holds that God wills just treatment for *all* people, irrespective of religious affiliation. Part of incarnating the Gospel message is to pursue this vision in practical expression.

Whether or not we respect the rights of other religious believers is clearly linked to our view of their religious beliefs. If non-Christian belief is viewed as culpable, moral rebellion against God, as the reconstructionalists do, then it is clearly very difficult to support a system that enshrines an educational right to hold these beliefs. If, however, non-Christian belief is seen as being a tenable option for a rational, moral person, even if it is not true, then there is a basis for treating religious belief as a matter of legitimate dispute. If this is the case, it becomes unacceptable to expect the State to propagate one of these disputed belief systems in preference to any of the others. A recognition of the tenability of other people's beliefs and the disputed status of one's own are indispensable elements of the transformationalist position. The theory of knowledge developed in Chapter 6 gives a basis for such attitudes.

The Other Side of The Coin

So far, it has been argued that Evangelical Christians can, with integrity, use a 'work-with' approach to secular education based on the pluralist principle. However, were the case to be rested there, I would, rightly, be accused of compatibilism. The other side of the transformationalist strategy is the goal of 'the total translation of the discipline into its rightful place amongst the treasures of God's kingdom' (Nelson, 1987, page 339). How does the position I have been describing match up to this criterion?

First, it is important to remember that I have, in this book, engaged in a wholesale redefinition of the widely influential concept of education (see Parts I and II). I have done this because the current liberal consensus is quite unacceptable to Evangelical Christians. Therefore, I have reconstructed it in ways that are, I believe, consistent with Evangelical Christian commitment.

However, this has been done in a way that affirms the importance of respecting the rights of those with commitments different to my own, both Christian and non-Christian. The concept of secular education has, therefore, been reconstructed such that, I hope, it is still acceptable to them. I have not been reluctant to do this. I am motivated to do so by my Christian commitment to the importance of community harmony, and to a God who commands that justice be done to all people. Indeed, Christian belief is probably the *securest* foundation that can be found for the pluralist principle.

Second, a view of secular education has been described that gives it a limited role in relation to religion. This is a major departure from the 'evangelistic' zeal displayed by many professional (as they call themselves) religious educators who are advocates of secular education. This certainly has important functions that relate particularly to the need for those of differing religious commitments to be prepared for living alongside each other as fellow citizens. However, as far as I am concerned, the most fundamental and formative religious educational functions should be carried out within communities of faith. Here, the constraints of the pluralist principle do not apply. The Christian nurture of the home and church is, therefore, of primary importance in the total educational process. Unlike many liberal educators, I do not see secular education as a panacea.

This leads to the third, probably most significant, way in which the position I have described differs fundamentally from that propounded by many of my colleagues involved in secular education. It concerns our attitude towards religious pluralism, and whether or not its existence is something to be celebrated, or regretted. A helpful starting point is John Hull's pamphlet *Mishmash* (1991a), in which he discusses the motives that lie behind opposition to multifaith religious education. His central argument is that they are based on a fear that mixing religions in education will result in psychological contamination. Such opposition is, he argues, essentially based on a feeling of disgust at the idea of mixing cultures and identities that 'should' be kept apart, hence the need for boundaries to maintain purity. Encounter is dangerous. Contamination through contact is resisted. Hull describes the attitude as follows: 'I am holy . . . and you are holy, but the ground between us is unholy and we will contaminate each other through a harmful mingling of blood if we should meet' (page 38).

Hull's alternative is to see holiness not in maintaining the traditions, and the distinctions between them, but in overcoming these distinctions. So, he writes, 'the boundary which separates shall become the holy ground, the common ground, the mutuality of response and responsibility which makes us truly human.

Holiness is discovered through encounter' (page 38). For Hull, clearly pluralism is something to be celebrated. Without it, holy ground is lost.

The attitude described in this book is much more ambivalent towards the fact of religious pluralism. On the one hand, Evangelicals can embrace the benefits that accrue from living within a plural world.[7] Indeed, there is much to be gained from the process of encounter and co-operation with members of other faiths. Certainly, harmonious community life, which Christians should value, cannot be achieved in a plural society without this. On the other hand, their belief in the exclusive message of the Gospel entails that, at the very same time, they will seek to undermine, through evangelism, the very pluralism that is providing them with these benefits. Put simply, they would like to see it replaced with something better. In a democratic society, all groups have the right, through persuasion, to seek to change the nature of their society. However, it has to be appreciated that this process of evangelism will never, in temporal terms, be completed, and any final Christian 'victory' can only be an eschatological vision. Pluralism, therefore, will always be a fact of Christian 'this-world' experience and will continue to provide its benefits, and its challenges. In secular education, this means that the pluralist principle will always apply. This ambivalence to religious pluralism is, in fact, a reflection of the Christian calling to be both in, but not of, a plural world. Being 'in the world' means that the secular nature of schooling can be embraced, but being 'not of the world' means that this secularity can never be treated as the ultimate ideal.

Any analogy that seeks to capture this ambivalence inevitably distorts it in some way. However, analogies can help, so I will try one here. If we think of Evangelicals as being involved in a 'post-Dunkirk' situation, this may help towards understanding their approach to pluralism. In those times, the British people experienced far from ideal circumstances. However, in some ways there were benefits to be gained from living under pressure. For example, it is part of human nature to respond with unusual qualities of spirit in adverse circumstances in a way that is not characteristic when life is less demanding. Furthermore, to experience a demanding situation can be a stimulus to personal maturity, which a more ideal way of life does not necessarily offer.

It is also the case that living in less than ideal circumstances may, quite properly, lead us to do things that are, in some sense, at odds with our own beliefs. For example, people for whom killing is abhorrent kill in wars. They regret the fact, but, in the circumstances that apply at such times, they can see no other option. Brian Walsh described this as following the most redemptive action possible.[8] He cites the issuing of sterile needles to drug addicts by a Christian medical mission in Canada as an example of such action. Many doctors have to face similar decisions. To amputate a limb is never something that a doctor would *wish* to do, but, in some circumstances, it is the most redemptive action possible. The ideal, of course, is the full health of the patient. To refuse to amputate on the grounds that the patient will never again be able to enjoy a full, able-bodied lifestyle would however, be callous in the extreme. In many of the circumstances life throws up, the only right course of action available is less desirable than would be wished in the ideal. For the Christian, this is an inescapable fact of life in a fallen world.

Returning again to our post-Dunkirk analogy, it is obvious that few people then wanted to perpetuate or celebrate the circumstances that pertained at that time. Rather, they had their sights fixed on, and actively worked towards, the D-Day experience. For Evangelicals, there is a 'D-Day' ahead, when all people will recognize Jesus Christ as Lord. This eschatological vision inspires them in their *current* experience of a plural world. In this sense, we can agree with Newbigin when he describes Christians as subversives, or undercover agents (1991, pages 81–3), looking to achieve a radical change in their current circumstances. However, this terminology is not meant to condone the use of immoral or unjust means in the realization of the eschatological vision. The Gospel must always be shared in a way that is appropriate to its message. Nor should it be taken to imply that we do not actively seek to achieve the best possible good in our current circumstances. As a gift from God, life should be lived to its best, even in the post-Dunkirk experience.

The purpose of my Dunkirk analogy has then been to make three points about the Christian's experience of living in a religiously plural world. First, even though it may be less than the ideal, there are still quite considerable benefits to be derived from the experience. There are things that I value about living in a plural society. Second, the fact that we are in less than ideal circumstances means that the only consistently Christian action may be less than the ideal because it is the most redemptive given current circumstances. Third, part of Christian mission will be to seek to change society through encouraging others to accept the Christian Gospel. Therefore, evangelism is a threat to pluralism.

However the use of this war-time analogy will not have been helpful if it has given the impression that I wish to treat the existence of religious pluralism as a warfare situation. I most certainly do not. Neither do I wish to suggest that Christians and members of other faiths are to view each other as enemies. However, I am seeking to accept the fact that deeply held differences of religious belief present a challenge that, if not faced in a realistic manner, poses a serious threat to the stability of society. As a matter of fact members of different religions sometimes do find each others' beliefs offensive.

The analogy has a limited purpose only. It is meant to illustrate how it is possible for Christians to embrace a situation that is less than the ideal in a way that allows them to appreciate the positive benefits of the situation while, at the same time, desiring, and actively working for, a change in the direction of more ideal circumstances. For the Evangelical Christian, religious pluralism can never be celebrated as the ideal, but it can be experienced as a situation that offers positive outcomes. Living an ethical life in the midst of it may demand that we do things that are less than our ideal in order to fulfil our Christian responsibility to carry out the most redemptive actions possible. To achieve fairness and community harmony in the secular educational system of a plural democracy, means giving space to religious beliefs that we believe to be untrue. This entails accepting restraints on our theological visions because, if we do not exercise such restraints, we will perpetuate unjust treatment of other people. In other, less constrained contexts, Evangelicals will, as appropriate, actively seek to persuade others to embrace the Christian Gospel. In the end, such action can only undermine religious pluralism. In a total revival situation, this could even be to the degree that the pluralist principle becomes redundant, secular education becomes unnecessary and education built on a Christian worldview becomes appropriate for all!

Finally, it has to be pointed out that, in seeking to interact with secular education, there will be limits beyond which an

Evangelical theology cannot go and still remain true to itself. To use a biblical picture, no one can serve two masters. Support for secular education must come from the believer's theological master. Once education calls one to abandon this loyalty, then a choice has to be made as to which to serve.

Stephen Neill has provided an interesting parallel to this situation in relation to mission (1980). He distinguishes between customs that cannot be tolerated if Christian belief is to remain true to itself as it seeks to contextualize with different cultures, and those that can be tolerated with integrity. The former include idolatry, female infanticide, and ritual prostitution, and the latter, polygamy, tribalism, and culturally specific ways of worshipping. If secular education continues to rely on a rationale derived from radical Christian liberalism, then I believe it has put itself in the first category as far as Evangelical Christians are concerned. There are limits to the restraints that can be exercised.

Some Objections

To conclude, it may be helpful if I briefly reply to a few of the commonest objections made to the position that I have been proposing.

First, there are some who feel that to give any credence to religious pluralism is necessarily to embrace relativism, and undermine the status of Christianity as uniquely true. However, this objection ignores two fundamental issues. First, it assumes that there are only two possible assessments that can be made of a religion, namely that it is either true or false. However, there is a third important option: a religion can be tenable, while still being false. By this I mean that I can agree that it is rational that a person hold to such beliefs, although I personally consider them to be false. It is this tenability of the many different forms of religious belief that makes religion a matter of dispute, and a subject on which reasonable people may differ. To acknowledge that the State has no right to make judgements on the truth of particular religious beliefs, is only to recognize their tenability. It is not an endorsement of relativism, but simply a recognition of their disputed status in society.

The second objection is to the attempt to create a secular middle ground. Education can never be neutral, it is argued; any attempt to make it so implicitly endorses secularism. Arthur Jones, headteacher of an independent Christian school, puts it like this:

> Over the centuries the Protestant churches have gradually surrendered the public sphere to control by secular assumptions and have survived by retreating into the private sector. On the face of it, this has seemed to be the ideal solution to the problem of how a society can maintain civil liberties amidst a diversity of cultures, of how the church can coexist with pagan ideologies. But there is a fundamental problem. If the private realm is characterised by groups with their own specific communal values, then what controls the public interactions? If there is no agreed public morality, no shared beliefs about the truth, then the outcome in the public realm will be exploitation or at least domination. (1992, page 127)

However, this analysis assumes that public, shared values *have* to be drawn from within particular communities. The only alternative Jones presents is a values vacuum into which a powerful lobby steps to achieve domination. The choice is between my values or someone else's. However, there is no reason why the values of the public community cannot be of a different order to those that bind faith communities together. In particular, I have suggested that a concern for harmony and community, the development of a common vision of the common good, and agreement on the articles of peace that are to govern life in the public sector can all provide a very strong base of community values. These values are all the stronger because they are created by negotiation, not imposed. Jones' suggestion really spells the death of public life because he seems to assume *either* a values vacuum, *or* a particular religious value base as the *only* options. He is right that the former leads to domination, but then so does the latter. The consensus that made Christian values a viable basis for public life has long since disappeared. True, the veneer still remains—prayers in Parliament, an established church, and so on—but public life cannot be built on a veneer especially as it becomes thinner by the day. To attempt this can only lead to conflict. If it is imposed using legal force, it will marginalize many minority communities, and lead to resistance from the secular majority.

Jones will reply that the strategy I propose privatizes faith. In one sense, it does, because constraints on my theological vision do have to be accepted. However, in a much more significant sense, it does not. People active in the public domain have two types of commitment. The first is to these secular, public values, and to the code of conduct agreed on the basis of them. The second is to their own religious faith. The latter is primary. It is these religious values that provide the theological rationale, and support, for the secular values. Therefore, they are essential to public, secular life. As Os Guinness puts it:

> The fact that the different religious roots of the public philosophy are largely invisible does not mean that they are unimportant or that public philosophy is secular in a secularist sense. On the contrary, a cut flower public philosophy will not work. So the health of the public philosophy depends . . . on the private cultivation of the first principles of the public philosophy within each home and faith community. (1991, page 45)

The crucial question is to do with authority. Even though I may, in some circumstances, treat religious values as private, I still accord them absolute and final authority. One might call this pragmatic privatization. The problem with secularism is that it radically privatizes religious values by claiming the absolute authority for the secular.

The third objection is to challenge my claim that the approach to public policy proposed in this book is non-discriminatory between religions. In my arguments, I have supported the principle of 'respect for the autonomy of the school classroom' (Leahy, 1990, page 142). Clearly, some theologies will not be able to accept this—for example the reconstructionalist position (see Chapter 7). Is my position not, then, exactly the same as that of John Hull? (See chapter 4.)

This objection does not take account of the very different nature of the criterion that excludes a particular theology in our two cases. Hull's position ends up proposing a civic theology that has a transcendental justification. It is one that rational people must accept, and offers an absolute definition of the good life. In my case, the only theologies that are barred from active participation in the public domain are those that cannot accept the pluralist principle. In other words, they are not prepared to accept the ethical principle that, in a plural society, State-sponsored secular education should not favour any one religion. They are not prepared to work with adherents from religions other than their own. Such theologies, therefore, are a threat to community harmony. Their exclusion is necessary for the health of society. Thus, it is a pragmatic decision. They can hardly complain that this is unfair when they are not prepared to support the principle of fairness themselves. A coalition cannot be expected to embrace those whose primary purpose is to undermine the coalition.

The fourth objection is to argue that my position is naive. Like the hunter eaten by the bear (see page 109), it does not take seriously the fact that the religions are, at heart, a threat to each other. Such overt co-operation is inevitably compromising. It does not recognize the powerful influences that are at work in schools that are not grounded in Christian principles. So, Stephen Perks says that for Christian parents to place their children in State schools 'is a denial of the faith and treason against God' (1992, page 129). Some would say the same to Christian teachers who work in them, that their energies would be better devoted to pursuing explicitly Christian goals. Secularism in any form is corrosive of true faith and, therefore, we should minimize our co-operation with it.

There are a number of points to make against such a position. First, it is dependent on the two humanities view, which demonizes all non-Christians, and their work. It seems to me that a more biblical position is that the hand of God can be discerned, to varying degrees, in the life of *all* people (see page 160). Certainly, in the State schools that I know, I see many good and positive things, which I can endorse and welcome as a Christian.

Second, I would still maintain that this view places too high an emphasis on the role of schooling. Children need to grow up appreciating their responsibilities as citizens, and having gained a certain amount of knowledge. This, essentially, is the limited function of State schools, where children learn to render unto Caesar what is Caesar's. No more. This objection underestimates the importance of the faith-based, often informal, education that is the province of the home and faith community. The worrying thing is that concern for children is often a low priority with churches, taking its place behind Bible studies, prayer gatherings, evangelistic events, and business meetings.

Perhaps the most alarming thing about this objection is the implication that Christians are called to live in a safe world, free of all threats of compromise. It represents the attempt to create a sanitized environment. However, such a world is not only free of compromise, it is also free of the opportunities for ministry. This is a denial of our call to incarnate Christ in a fallen world. How would we feel about a Christian who argued that involvement in relief work was wrong because it is impossible to help all those in need? He might argue that to decide to feed one person and to let someone else die, a decision that inevitably has to be made, is to compromise Christian faith. The refusal to work in education alongside those of other faiths because it entails the risk of compromise seems, to me, to be on the same level.

What my critics do rightly remind me is that I should never be complacent about the values children are exposed to in school. There are secular educators who will abuse the trust put in them by faith communities. Like the frog in the water with the rising temperature, there may come a time when we must jump out, but it is very easy to be caught unawares. The secular domain poses a threat as well as an opportunity.

The final objection focuses on the value of involving oneself in such a limited activity as secular education. Surely, it is said, there are projects of far greater eternal significance than the promotion of conversation between religious communities?

There are two responses to this. First, in the world as it actually is, the most redemptive act possible in educational terms is to contribute to this secular educational ideal. The only other option is to withdraw from it. As Christians we have a calling to be in the thick of the business of redemption, not shouting from the sidelines.

Second, this view underestimates the impact for good that successful secular education can have. If children left school able to listen to and learn from others, aware of the fundamental significance of religion, and able to reflect intelligently on their own commitments, the world would be in a better state than it is today. Certainly, adults like that would be far more open to the Gospel message than are most in the Britain of the 1990s.[9]

Postscript

COMMITMENT IS A fact of life; to be human is to be committed. One of the major problems that our race faces is that we cannot agree on what these commitments should be. The differences are particularly strongly felt when it comes to religion.

This one fact poses the biggest threat to the success of any enterprise that seeks to integrate theology and schooling. The greatest difficulty is to avoid the situation where the commitments of one powerful grouping are foisted on everyone else. This is all the more invidious when it is done in the name of rationality. It is so easy, for example, for the humanist to assume that we can *all* agree that what *really* matters is the moral teaching of a religion, or that agnosticism is *clearly* the strongest basis for good relations between the religions. All of us are inclined to feel that, if only everyone could be like me, then all the problems of pluralism would dissolve. However, the missionary zeal of the humanist, the Evangelical Christian, and the radical Christian liberal are all equally inappropriate in the secular classroom. We can sympathize with the attempt of the Indian Government to stem the tide of Hindu fanaticism that wishes to make being truly Indian conditional on being Hindu. We, in the West, have to be aware of our tendency to make being rational dependent on the holding of particular commitments.

In the face of the problems, it is not surprising that many countries ban religion altogether from the classroom. To do this, however, is to miss a great opportunity. In the week that I write this postscript, the tenth anniversary celebrations of the first multifaith syllabus of religious education for Bradford are taking place. The local paper, the *Telegraph and Argus*, reports the comments of one participant as follows:

> People from Bradford's five faiths . . . engaged together in nine months' hard work, including many evenings of study and careful listening, argument and clarification. It was only

when we were able to face the important and strongly held differences between the faith groups that we really began to progress to the deeper commonalities. Then respect became real. Friendships across the religions were forged that stand today. (1993, page 21)

To run away from religious differences is to miss such an opportunity. The task our schools have is to look these differences in the face and help children live with them in a way that builds our community life, and respects the integrity of the faith groups. Teachers who seek either to evangelize their students, or to deconstruct their theology and replace it with something more rational, are a threat to harmony, and are abusing the trust invested in them by the community.

As an Evangelical Christian, I have had to work through my own response to this. My prayer is that my struggles may be of some help to other teachers. We all face the same question—'how can I handle my commitment responsibly?' Diversity within unity is not going to be promoted by teachers who think that this question is someone else's problem.

NOTES

Chapter 1

1. This material is taken from the address given by Archbishop Habgood at the conference 'RE: The Way Ahead' on 29 June, 1992. The Conference Proceedings are available from the Culham College Institute, 60 East St Helen Street, Abingdon, Oxfordshire OX14 5EB.
2. This is a shorthand and, inevitably, simplistic summary of the complicated Education Acts of 1988 and 1993. However, it does reflect the aspiration of many of the influential figures behind the legislation. For an alternative viewpoint, see John Hull (1989).
3. By describing religious pluralism as a fact, I am simply pointing to the inescapable existence of a massive number of religious options, both between and within particular religions. The mass media and increased movement of people around the world means that our generation is more aware of this pluralism than ever before. I am not, however, endorsing any particular theology of pluralism. Indeed, I have many reasons to differ from what has traditionally been described as the pluralist option in Christian theologies of other religions (see Chapter 3).
4. I use the phrase 'common schools' here to describe those schools that are maintained by the State and whose educational credo is not built on a specifically religious vision. Their mission is to provide an education that is appropriate and acceptable to all students and their families, irrespective of their religious background. These are sometimes called county schools to distinguish them from church voluntary schools and independent schools. I have chosen not to use these latter terms because there are a number of church schools, mainly Anglican ones, and many independent schools that would aspire to the mission of the common school. Furthermore, as increasing numbers of schools become grant maintained, the term county school will appear anachronistic.

   Common schools are also called secular schools. This is an important and useful term, but I have chosen not to use it at this point as I wish to discuss it in some detail later.
5. The phenomenological approach is a term used within religious education to denote an academic or descriptive approach. It has its

origins in the work of Professor Ninian Smart at Lancaster University. Its early definitive statement was in the Schools Council Working Paper, number 36, 'RE in Secondary Schools', published in 1971. For a more recent and critical discussion, see Michael Grimmitt (1987a), especially pages 40–6 and 209–13.

6. The term 'liberal educational values' denotes a consensus that has dominated the theory of education since the 1960s. The main features of this are a commitment to open, critical rationality, and to democratic principles. There are, however, many different, detailed interpretations. For a brief, but excellent, summary, see McLaughlin (1992c).

7. In using the term 'stage defenders', Hull is drawing on theories of faith development. These suggest that maturity in faith commitment advances as people progress through certain clearly definable stages. A stage defender is someone who resists such progress and, therefore, remains at a less mature stage of development. For further details of faith development theories, see Astley (1991), and Astley and Francis (1992).

8. Hull's passionate critique of these people's attitudes (1991a) is well worth reading. I shall, however, argue in due course that he has failed to take account of some valid theological objections, preferring to present their position as rooted in nothing more than fear of contamination by other religions.

9. So influential, in fact, that it was a major factor in determining the wording of the religious education and worship clauses of the 1988 Education Act. It continues to exert considerable influence in Parliamentary consideration of these subjects. For example, early in 1993, John Patten, the then Secretary of State for Education, made a speech in which he argued that Christian teaching in schools will be the way to improve the moral life of the nation. Similarly, in 1992, Lady Olga Maitland set up the organization Christian Call to campaign for a return to Christian-based religious education.

10. See also Deakin (1989), where similar arguments are put forward in support of State funding for faith-based schools. Deakin argues that, in a religiously pluralist society, democratic principles entail that faith communities should have access to State-financed schooling that accords with their tradition. She denies that education for all in common schools is adequate, on the grounds that it is inevitably secular and, therefore, antireligious. Thus, a Bill introduced into the House of Lords by Baroness Cox in November, 1990, sought funding for those independent schools that 'cater for families who would normally expect to use the State system of education, but who seek a less secular environment than that

found within the usual State school'. See also Thiessen (1985), and Roques (1989).

Chapter 2

1. Hirst's major writings spanned the period from early in 1960 to mid 1985. He was a member of the Swann Committee, which produced the influential report *Education for All* on race and education. Although his arguments are now widely criticized, his conclusions on the autonomy of rational knowledge and of education are still very influential. I do not criticize his arguments in depth here. Detailed discussions of his views on theology and education can be found in Hull (1976), Russell (nd), Cooling (1984), Thiessen (1985 and 1987), Francis (1990a and 1990b), McLaughlin (1992a), and Hughes (1992). For the purposes of my argument, all that is necessary at this point is to note the influence of his ideas in the development of religious education theory.

2. Tasos Kazepides (1982 and 1983) has pursued the logic of this Hirstian position to its bitter end by arguing that the teaching of religious doctrine can never be part of education because it is outside the rational tradition.

3. Burtonwood's position is based on the writings of the philosopher of science Karl Popper, who argues that all knowledge is conjecture, which is open to refutation.

4. Most of my discussion of Grimmitt is based on his major work *Religious Education and Human Development* (1987a). Unless otherwise indicated, page references in this chapter refer to this book.

5. See, for example, Kazepides (1982), Rosenak (1982), Blake (1983), Callan (1985), Gardner (1988 and 1989), Attfield (1991), and the footnote on Hill (1990a, page 55).

6. Arlblaster (1984) offers a detailed analysis of the philosophy of liberalism, in which he argues that the liberty of the individual is its defining characteristic. White (1973), Attfield (1991), and Blake (1983) are examples of educational writers who explicitly employ it.

7. See Crittenden (1988) for a major discussion of these issues.

Chapter 3

1. The question of whether or not religious education should either challenge or confirm the religious identity of pupils is the subject of

much debate. See, for example, Hull (1991c), Meijer (1991), and Haussmann (1993).

2. Expounded most famously in *The Myth of God Incarnate* (1977), which he edited.

3. See, for example, Oldfield (1986, page 178), Watson (1987, page 35), and Hammond, *et al.* (1990, page 197).

4. Hick's most comprehensive statement of his position on pluralism comes in *An Interpretation of Religion* (1989). A useful summary is given in Hick (1988).

5. For discussions of the two absolutist traditions of Christian theology, inclusivism and exclusivism, see Race (1983), Hick (1985, Chapter 3, and 1988, pages 365–77), D'Costa (1986), and Driver (1987).

6. This section does not constitute a comprehensive critique of Hick's pluralist theology. It is limited to a consideration of its emotivist implications and prescriptive nature. For a more detailed discussion, see D'Costa (1986), and Netland (1991).

7. For a full discussion of the conflict between religious doctrines, see Christian (1972).

8. Page references in this chapter are to Runzo's 1986 work *Reason, Relativism and God*, unless otherwise stated.

9. See note 5, Chapter 1, for a discussion of the phenomenological method.

10. See Hammond, *et al.* (1990).

11. For example, Grimmitt suggests that the educational worth of a religion can be judged by the degree to which it promotes humanization.

12. See, for example, my discussion of Runzo's support for the absolute truth of relativism on pages 40–5. Runzo also gives the principle of non-contradiction as another example of such a criterion (page 185).

13. See Hill (1990b) for a full discussion of religious relativism and education.

Chapter 4

1. Page references in this section are to *Moral Education in a Secular Society* (1974b), unless otherwise indicated.

2. Page references in this chapter are to *Studies in Religion and Education* (1984), unless otherwise indicated.

3. See Netland (1991, pages 180–95) for a discussion of these tools of rational thought.

4. See Thatcher (1990, page 79), Francis (1990a, page 32, and 1990b, page 360) for further discussion of this point.

5. For examples of writers who take the line that to be religious is to have ultimate commitments, see Thiessen (1982), Hill (1985b), Totterdell (1988), and Newbigin (1989).
6. This is an important point because the case for the public funding of Christian schools is built on this argument, for example, Walsh and Middleton (1984), Neuhaus (1987), Roques (1989), and Deakin (1989). Supporting evidence, in the form of rulings from American courts that secular humanism is to count as a religion (Thiessen, 1982, page 60, and Newbigin, 1989, page 94) is often cited.

Chapter 5

1. See Cooling (1990b) for the article and Benson (1990) for the letter.
2. Taken from the introduction to the book he edited, *The Gospel and Contemporary Culture* (1992).
3. Antony Stanton, then RE adviser in Kent, said in an address at the London University Institute of Education on 16 February, 1981, that 'the new RE proceeds logically from radical liberal theology'. Here he means the tradition of theology associated with writers such as Rudolph Bultmann, David Jenkins, and Don Cupitt.
4. These ideas are developed further in the article I wrote entitled 'Professionalism Confessionalism and Religious Education' (1993).
5. See Hamnet (1990, pages 6–7), and Netland (1991, Chapter 1), for a fuller development of this point.
6. The National Curriculum Council's *Analysis of Agreed Syllabuses for Religious Education* (1993) made this point. The Scottish guidelines, *Religious and Moral Education 5–14* (1992) and the *School Curriculum and Assessment Authority's Model RE Syllabuses* (1994), also emphasize respect and understanding. The core syllabus of religious education for Northern Ireland supports the 'Education for Mutual Understanding' initiative, which is designed to improve relations between the two communities of the Province.

Chapter 6

1. In this chapter, I will be developing a view of religious knowledge that Brian Hill (1990b) calls a 'literal–persuasive' view. He offers this as an alternative to the relativistic views, which he argues have heavily influenced religious education.
2. Polanyi's most important work is *Personal Knowledge*, first published in 1958, then a revised edition in 1962. His *The Tacit Dimension* (1967) is a helpful, brief introduction to his thought, as is Drusilla Scott's more substantial *Everyman Revisited* (1985).

Polanyi's ideas are gaining popular appeal through the works of Lesslie Newbigin (for example 1989) and the 'Gospel and Our Culture' movement.

3. For further development of the role of presuppositions in science, see works by Ronald Laura, Michael Leahy, and Elmer Thiessen listed in the Bibliography, pages 191 and 194.

4. I am indebted to Elmer Thiessen for the notion of normal autonomy (1991 and 1993).

5. Here, and in the rest of this chapter, I am drawing on the work of the American philosophers of religion Alvin Plantinga, and Nicholas Wolterstorff. Details of their writings are included in the Bibliography, pages 193 and 195.

6. See Note 5, Chapter 3, page 180, for references on exclusivism and inclusivism. See Race (1983, pages 43–50) for further comments.

7. See Netland (1991, pages 183–6) for a discussion of criteria for assessment that are independent of belief.

8. A good example of this is to be found in Richard Lindley's article in *Education* (1992). The influential book from the Religious Experience Research Unit (Hammond, *et al.*, 1990) is a systematic attempt to avoid controversial religious experience by focusing on universal spiritual experience. I deal with this issue as it affects science education in an article in the *British Journal of Religious Education* (1990a).

9. The important distinction in any realist theory of religious knowledge is between what finite human beings know, and what is known by the mind of God. The former aspires to the latter, but is never the same as it.

10. A similar view of interfaith relations is developed in a paper by the Church's Commission for Inter-Faith Relations, Religious Education Group (1993).

Chapter 7

1. The issue of the nature and purpose of church schools is a complicated one. Roman Catholic schools generally see themselves as distinctively Christian, while Anglican schools may not. For further information and a range of views, see O'Keeffe (1986), Lankshear (1992), and Marsh (1992).

2. At the time of writing, there is no one, main source of information on the philosophy underlying the Christian Schools movement. Helpful treatments include Deakin (1989), Jones (1992), McLaughlin (1992c), O'Keeffe (1992), and Thiessen (1993).

Further information is available from the following organizations: Christians in Education, 53 Romney Street, London SW1P 3RF

Christian Schools Trust, c/o 8 Ascension Road, Chase Cross, Romford, Essex RM5 3RS

Oak Hill Trust, 16 Cotham Park, Brentry, Bristol BS6 6BU.

3. Readers are referred back to the quotation on page 7, which started the book. A more detailed treatment follows in Chapter 8.

4. More detailed criticisms of this approach can be found on pages 134–137.

5. For a detailed treatment of this view of the State, see Skillen (1990).

6. I consider this to be the main mistake John Hull makes in his brilliant monograph *Mishmash* (1991a). He rightly exposes the unacceptable tribalism of some Christian thinking, but fails to take seriously the fact that religious pluralism *also* creates a legitimate theological problem.

7. I am here picking up John Hull's distinction between the illuminating and adjudicating roles that theology can play. See page 53.

Chapter 8

1. See Marsden (1987) for a detailed description of the changes that have taken place at Fuller Theological Seminary. These reflect the changes in the wider Evangelical world. Readers are also referred to the leaflet 'Who do Evangelicals think they are?', published by the Evangelical Alliance at 186 Kennington Park Road, London SE11 4BT.

2. The most recent, systematic treatment of education from the reconstructionalist perspective by a British writer is Stephen Perks' (1992) book.

3. The Evangelical Alliance leaflet (see Note 1 above) includes a table listing the differences between this fundamentalist position and that of the Evangelicals.

4. Perks is exceptional in addressing this question directly. His position is that the role of the State is restricted to ensuring that justice prevails in society. He interprets this as meaning that the State has no business in interfering with education, which is a family responsibility. For an extensive treatment offering an Evangelical Christian view of the State's role see *Pluralisms and Horizons* (Mouw & Griffioen 1993).

Chapter 9

1. Many of Hill's articles have appeared in the *Journal of Christian Education*. Recent books have included *The Greening of Christian Education* (1985a), *That They May Learn* (1990a), and *Values Education in Australian Schools* (1988). Unfortunately, none of

these are readily available in the UK. Of his articles, two of the most significant, from the point of view of this book, are 1985c and 1985d.

2. For Hill's criticisms of radical Christian liberalism, see particularly his 1985c and 1990b articles.

3. See Derek Meakin's two articles (1979 and 1988) for a helpful discussion of the relationship between knowledge of options, choice, autonomy, and education.

4. Here, Hill is drawing on Paul's description of the human dilemma in Romans 7. He discusses this on page 28 of *Faith At The Blackboard* (1982).

5. Hill is unclear on his position here. Thus, in *The Greening of Christian Education* (1985a), he seems to deny that nurture and evangelism are educational activities, but, in *That They May Learn* (1990a), they are included in a glossary of educational terms as being related Christian terms.

6. He is also concerned about the sectarian implications of such schools. See his 1989 article for an exposition of his views.

Chapter 10

1. See, for example, Hick (1977) and Hick and Knitter (1987).

2. Examples of the writers I would cite are Arthur Holmes, Alvin Plantinga, Nicholas Wolterstorff, and Brian Hill. See the Bibliography for details.

3. Many Evangelicals have been involved in the 'Gospel and Our Culture' movement, which is inspired by Newbigin's work.

4. See Hill (1985c, 1986, and 1993).

5. Perhaps the best example is the establishment of the Tear Fund (The Evangelical Alliance Relief Fund) in 1968. It is now the twenty-fifth largest charity in Britain.

6. I am here referring to Burn and Hart's, *The Crisis in Religious Education*, which appeared as the 1988 Education Bill was passing throughParliament,andwaswidelycirculatedamongMPsandPeers.

7. The benefits were discussed in Chapter 6.

8. This example was shared with me in a conversation at a meeting of Christians in Education.

9. Ian Barns, Lecturer in the Institute of Science and Technology Policy at Murdoch University in Perth, Australia, made the following helpful suggestion to me. 'The preaching of the gospel thus both requires and creates the conditions of public dialogical open-ness through which people can freely hear, consider, and respond to the claims of Christ, either by acceptance or rejection . . . Rather than the secularity of public life being based on the supposed autonomy of secular reason, it will be seen to be contingent upon the conditions of communicative freedom required by the logic of gospel preaching itself.'

BIBLIOGRAPHY

The following abbreviations are used:

BJES   *British Journal of Educational Studies*
BJRE   *British Journal of Religious Education*
JCE   *Journal of Christian Education*
JPE   *Journal of Philosophy of Education*

Ali Ashraf, Syed, 'A View of Education: An Islamic Perspective', in O'Keeffe, Bernadette, ed., *Schools For Tomorrow: Building Walls or Building Bridges*. Falmer Press, 1988.

Alves, Rubem, *Protestantism and Repression*. SCM Press, 1985.

Anderson, Norman, *Christianity and World Religions*. InterVarsity Press, 1984.

AREAI, *Religious Education for Ages 5 to 16/18*. St Martins College, 1989.

Arlblaster, Anthony, *The Rise and Decline of Western Liberalism*. Basil Blackwell, 1984.

Arthur, Chris, *Biting the Bullet*. The Saint Andrew Press, 1990.

Aspin, David, 'Critical Openness as a Platform For Diversity—Towards an Ethic of Belonging', in O'Keeffe, Bernadette, ed., *Schools for Tomorrow: Building Walls or Building Bridges*. Falmer Press, 1988.

Astley, Jeff, 'Theology and Curriculum Selection', *BJRE*, 1988, Vol. 10:2, pages 86–91.

——, *How Faith Grows*. National Society/Church House Publishing, 1991.

——, and Francis, Leslie, eds., *Christian Perspectives on Faith Development*. Gracewing, 1992.

Attfield, D. G., 'The Challenge of the Education Reform Act to Church Schools', *BJRE*, 1991, vol 13:3, pages 136–42.

Barclay, Oliver, *Developing A Christian Mind*. InterVarsity Press, 1984.

Bates, Dennis, 'Developing RE in Topic-based Approaches to Learning', in Bastide, Derek, ed., *Good Practice in Primary Religious Education, 4–11*. Falmer Press, 1992.

Bebbington, David, *Evangelicalism in Modern Britain*. Unwin Hyman, 1989.

Bibliography

Benson, Ian, 'Fervent Response', *Junior Education*, December, 1990, page 19.

Biggar, Nigel, 'Attesting the Evangel Evangelically', *Spectrum*, 1989, vol. 21:1, pages 27–37.

Blake, Nigel, 'Church Schools, RE and the Multi-Ethnic Community: a reply to D. Aspin', *JPE*, 1983, vol. 17:2, pages 241–50.

Brown, Colin, 'The Concept of Evangelical', *Churchman*, 1981, vol. 95:2, pages 104–9.

Browning, Robert, 'Befriending the World: Beyond Inter-faith Dialogue to Action', *Religious Education*, 1990, vol. 85:3, pages 331–45.

Burn, John, and Hart, Colin, *The Crisis in Religious Education*. The Educational Research Trust, 1988.

Burtonwood, Neil, *The Culture Concept in Educational Studies*. NFER-Nelson, 1986.

Callan, Eamonn, 'McLaughlin on Parental Rights', *JPE*, 1985, vol. 19:1, pages 111–18.

——, 'Faith, Worship and Reason in Religious Upbringing', *JPE*, 1988, vol. 22:2, pages 183–93.

——, 'Godless Moral Education and Liberal Tolerance', *JPE*, 1989, vol. 23:2, pages 267–81.

CCIFR, *Mission, Dialogue and Inter Religious Encounter*. CCBI, 1993.

Chapman, Colin, *The Christian Message in a Multi-Faith Society*. Latimer House, 1992.

Christian, William, *Oppositions of Religious Doctrines*. MacMillan, 1972.

Christian Herald, 'Fight For Christian RE', 28 November, 1992.

Cook, David, 'Man In Society', in Wright, David, ed., *Essays in Evangelical Social Ethnics*. Paternoster Press, 1978.

Cooling, Trevor, *The Evangelical Christian and Religious Education*. Unpublished MA thesis, University of London, 1984.

——, 'Science and Religious Education—Conflict or Co-operation?', *BJRE*, 1990a, vol. 13:1, pages 35–42.

——, 'Performing Miracles', *Junior Education*, October, 1990b, pages 10–11.

——, 'Professionalism, Confessionalism and Religious Education', *Spectrum*, 1993, vol. 25:2, pages 129–45.

Cox, Edwin, *Problems and Possibilities for Religious Education*. Hodder & Stoughton, 1983.

Crittenden, Brian, *Parents, the State and the Right to Educate*. Melbourne, Australia, Melbourne University Press, 1988.

D'Costa, Gavin, *Theology and Religious Pluralism*. Basil Blackwell, 1986.

Deakin, Ruth, *Christian Schools—The Case for Public Funding*. Regius Press, 1989.

Bibliography

Department for Education, *Religious Education and Collective Worship—Circular 1/94.* DES, 1994.

Driver, Tom, 'The Case For Pluralism', in Hick, John, and Knitter, Paul, eds., *The Myth of Christian Uniqueness.* SCM Press, 1987.

Elkin, Susan, 'The Altar of Learning', *Education,* 11 December, 1992.

Francis, Leslie, 'The Logic of Education, Theology and the Church School', in Francis, Leslie, and Thatcher, Adrian, eds., *Christian Perspectives for Education.* Gracewing, 1990a.

——, 'Theology of Education', *BJES,* 1990b, vol. 38:4, pages 349–64.

Gardner, Peter, 'Religious Upbringing and the Ideal of Autonomy', *JPE,* 1988, vol. 22:1, pages 89–105.

——, 'Liberal Autonomy and Religious Upbringing'. Unpublished paper, 1989.

Gilkey, Langdon, 'Plurality and Its Theological Implications', in Hick, John, and Knitter, Paul, eds., *The Myth of Christian Uniqueness.* SCM Press, 1987.

Goldingay, John, 'How Far Do Readers Make Sense? Interpreting Biblical Narrative', *Themelios,* 1993, vol. 18:2, pages 5–10.

Grimmitt, Michael, *What Can I Do in RE?.* Mayhew-McCrimmon, 1978.

——, 'When Is Commitment a Problem in Religious Education?', *BJES,* 1981, vol. 29:1, pages 42–53.

——, 'World Religions and Personal Development', in Jackson, Robert, ed., *Approaching World Religions.* John Murray, 1982.

——, *Religious Education and Human Development.* McCrimmons, 1987a.

——, 'Religious Education and Value Assumptions', *BJRE,* 1987b, vol. 9:3, pages 160–70.

——, 'The Use of Religious Phenomena in Schools: some theoretical and practical considerations', *BJRE,* 1991, vol. 13:2, pages 77–88.

——, et al., *A Gift to the Child: Religious Education in the Primary School.* Simon & Schuster, 1991.

Guinness, Os, 'Tribespeople, Idiots or Citizens?: Evangelicals, Religious Liberty and a Public Philosophy for the Public Square'. Unpublished paper, 1989.

——, Tribespeople, Idiots or Citizens?: Religious Liberty and the Reforging of the American Public Philosophy', *Spectrum,* 1991, vol. 23:1, pages 29–50.

Gunton, Colin, 'Knowledge and Culture: towards an epistemology of the concrete', in Montefiore, Hugh, ed., *The Gospel and Contemporary Culture.* Mowbray, 1992.

Hammond, John, *et al.*, *New Methods in RE Teaching.* Oliver & Boyd, 1990.

Hamnet, Ian, *Religious Pluralism and Unbelief.* Routledge, 1990.

Haussmann, Werner, 'Walking in Other People's Moccasins?', *BJRE*, 1993, vol. 15:2, pages 12–22.

Helm, Paul, ed., *Objective Knowledge*. InterVarsity Press, 1987.

Hesselgrave, David, and Rommen, Edward, *Contextualization: Meanings, Methods and Models*. Apollos, 1989.

Hick, John, ed., *The Myth of God Incarnate*. SCM Press, 1977.

——, *Problems of Religious Pluralism*. MacMillan, 1985.

——, 'Religious Pluralism and Salvation', *Faith and Philosophy*, 1988, vol. 5:4, pages 365–77.

——, *An Interpretation of Religion*. MacMillan, 1989.

——, and Knitter, Paul, eds., *The Myth of Christian Uniqueness*. SCM Press, 1987.

Hill, Brian, 'Scriptural Principles of Earthly Citizenship', *JCE*, 1963, vol. 6:1, pages 7–16.

——, 'The Origin of Man: Pointers for Christian Teachers and Counsellors', *JCE*, 1965a, vol. 8:1, pages 22–30.

——, 'Must Christians Indoctrinate?', *JCE*, 1965b, vol. 8:3, pages 136–44.

——, 'Education to Meet the Challenge of the Times', *JCE*, 1970, vol. 13:3, pages 153–68.

——, *Called To Teach: The Christian Presence in Australian Education*. Sydney, Australia, Angus & Robertson, 1971.

——, *Education and the Endangered Individual*. New York Teachers' College Press, 1973.

——, 'Religious Instruction: An Anachronism', *JCE*, 1974, Papers 50, pages 35–45.

——, 'Subjectivity and Subject Matter in Teaching', *JCE*, 1978a, Papers 62, pages 3–10.

——, 'Is It Time We De-Schooled Christianity?', *JCE*, 1978b, Papers 63, pages 5–21.

——, 'Education For Commitment: A Logical Contradiction', *Journal of Educational Thought*, 1981, vol. 15:3, pages 159–70.

——, *Faith At The Blackboard*. Michigan, Eerdmans, 1982.

——, 'Going Into All the World of Education', *JCE*, 1983, Papers 77, pages 38–50.

——, *The Greening of Christian Education*. New South Wales, Australia, Lancer, 1985a.

——, 'Religion, Hobby or Habitat?', *JCE*, 1985b, Papers 84, pages 3–5.

——, 'In Another World: Educational Responses to Modern Pluralism', *JCE*, 1985c, Papers 84, pages 21–33.

——, 'Values Education in a Secular Democracy', *Journal of the Indian Council for Philosophical Research*, 1985d, vol. 3, pages 65–79.

——, 'The Voices of Revelation and Science', *JCE*, 1985e, Papers 82, pages 3–5.

Bibliography

——, 'The Educational Needs of the Children of Expatriates', *Missiology: An International Review*, 1986, vol. 14:3, pages 325–46.

——, *Choosing The Right School*. Sydney, Australia, Australian Christian Teachers' Fellowship, 1987a.

——, 'The Potential of the Voluntary School Christian Group', *JCE*, 1987b, Papers 88, pages 55–63.

——, *Values Education in Australian Schools*. Murdoch, Australia, University of Murdoch, 1988.

——, 'Shall We Wind Down State Schools?', *Spectrum*, 1989, vol. 21:2, pages 131–43.

——, *That They May Learn*. Paternoster Press, 1990a.

——, 'Will and Should the Religious Studies Appropriate to Schools in a Pluralistic Society Foster Religious Relativism?', *BJRE*, 1990b, vol. 12:3, pages 126–36.

——, 'Transcultural Education: A Model for Expatriate Education', *JCE*, 1993, vol. 35:1, pages 29–47.

Hirst, Paul, 'Christian Education: a contradiction in terms?', *Learning for Living*, 1972, vol. 11:4, pages 6–11.

——, *Knowledge and the Curriculum*. Routledge & Kegan Paul, 1974a.

——, *Moral Education in a Secular Society*. University of London Press, 1974b.

——, 'Education, Catechesis and the Church School', *BJRE*, 1981, vol. 3:3, pages 85–93.

——, 'Education and Diversity of Belief', in Felderhof, M. C., ed., *Religious Education in a Pluralistic Society*. Hodder & Stoughton, 1985.

Hobbs, Maurice, *Teaching in a Multi-Racial Society*. Paternoster Press, 1987.

Hogan, Padraig, 'What Makes Practice Educational', *JPE*, 1990, vol. 24:1, pages 15–26.

Holmes, Arthur, *Contours of a Christian World View*. Michigan, Eerdmans, 1983.

Hughes, Fred, *What Do You Mean—Christian Education?*. Paternoster Press, 1992.

Hull, John, 'Christian Theology and Educational Theory: can there be connections?', *BJES*, 1976, vol. 24, pages 127–43.

——, 'Editorial', *BJRE*, 1980a, vol. 3:1, pages 1–2.

——, 'Editorial', *BJRE*, 1980b, vol. 3:2, pages 41–3.

——, 'Open Minds and Empty Hearts', in Jackson, Robert, ed., *Approaching World Religions*. John Murray, 1982.

——, *Studies in Religion and Education*. Falmer Press, 1984.

——, *What Prevents Christian Adults From Learning?* SCM Press, 1985a.

——, 'A Response to Karl-Ernst Nipkow', in Felderhof, M., ed.,

Religious Education in a Pluralistic Society. Hodder & Stoughton, 1985b.

——, *The Act Unpacked*. University of Birmingham/Christian Education Movement, 1989.

——, *Mishmash: Religious Education in a Multi-Cultural Britain*. University of Birmingham/Christian Education Movement, 1991a.

—— 'Human Development and Capitalist Society', in Fowler, James, *et al.*, ed., *Stages of Faith and Religious Development*. SCM Press, 1991b.

——, 'Editorial', *BJRE*, 1991c, vol. 13:2, pages 75–6.

——, *God-Talk with Young Children*. University of Birmingham/Christian Education Movement, 1991d.

——, 'Editorial', *BJRE*, 1992, vol. 14:2, pages 69–72.

Hulmes, Edward, 'Christian Education in a Multi-cultural Society', in McClelland, V., ed., *Christian Education in a Pluralist Society*. Routledge, 1988.

——, *Education and Cultural Diversity*. Longman, 1989.

Islamic Academy, *Swann Committee Report: An Evaluation From The Muslim Point of View*. Islamic Academy, 1985.

Jackson, Robert, 'The Concerns of Religious Education and the Characterization of Hinduism', *BJRE*, 1984, vol. 6:3, pages 141–6.

——, 'The Misrepresentation of Religious Education', in Leicester, M., and Taylor, M., eds., *Ethics, Ethnicity and Education*. Kogan Page, 1992.

Johns, Eric, 'The Unacceptable Aim of Religious Education', *BJRE*, 1981, vol. 4:1, pages 28–30.

Jones, Arthur, 'Christian Education Today: What Is It and How Can We Have It?', *Spectrum*, 1992, vol. 24:2, pages 125–41.

Jones, Malcolm, 'The Swann Report on "Education For All": a critique', *JPE*, 1986, vol. 20:1, pages 107–12.

——, 'Prejudice', in Haydon, Graham, ed., *Education For A Pluralist Society: Bedford Way Papers 30*. Institute of Education, University of London, 1987.

Kaufmann, Gordon, 'Religious Diversity, Historical Consciousness and Christian Theology', in Hick, John and Knitter, Paul, eds., *The Myth of Christian Uniqueness*. SCM Press, 1987.

Kazepides, Tasos, 'Educating, Socialising and Indoctrinating', *JPE*, 1982, vol. 16:2, pages 155–65.

——, 'Is RE Possible?: a rejoinder to W. D. Hudson', *JPE*, 1983, vol. 17:2, pages 259–65.

Kirk, Andrew, 'Theology For The Sake Of Mission', *Anvil*, 1990, vol. 7:1, pages 23–36.

Knitter, Paul, 'Towards a Liberation Theology of Religions', in Hick, John and Knitter Paul, eds., *The Myth of Christian Uniqueness*. SCM Press, 1987.

Bibliography

Kraft, Charles 'The Church in Culture—A Dynamic Equivalence Model', in Stott, John, and Coote, Robert, eds., *Down to Earth: Studies in Christianity and Culture*. Hodder & Stoughton, 1980.

Lakatos, Imre, 'Falsification and the Methodology of Scientific Research Programmes', in Lakatos, Imre, and Musgrave, Alan, eds., *Criticism and the Growth of Knowledge*. Cambridge University Press, 1970.

Lamb, Christopher, 'An Evangelical Theology of Pluralism: A Personal View', *Spectrum*, 1989, vol. 21:1, pages 19–26.

Lankshear, David, *A Shared Vision: Education in Church Schools*. National Society/Church House Publications, 1992.

Laura, Ronald, 'Philosophical Foundations of Religious Education', *Educational Theory*, 1978, vol. 28:4, pages 310–17.

——, and Leahy, Michael, 'Religious Upbringing and Rational Autonomy', *JPE*, 1989, vol. 23:2, pages 253–65.

Leahy, Michael, 'Indoctrination, Evangelization, Catechesis and Religious Education', *BJRE*, 1990, vol. 12:3, pages 137–44.

Leech, Alison, 'Another Look at Phenomenology and Religious Education', *BJRE*, 1989, vol. 11:2, pages 70–5.

Lewis, Terry, 'A House Divided'. St Vital, Manitoba, Canada, unpublished paper from Christian School Consultants, Inc., nd.

Lindley, Richard, 'The Common Factor', *Education*, 28 August, 1992.

Lloyd, Ieuan, 'Confession and Reason', *BJRE*, 1986, vol. 8:3, pages 140–5.

MacKay, Donald, 'Objectivity As A Christian Value', in Helm, Paul, ed., *Objective Knowledge: A Christian Perspective*. InterVarsity Press, 1987.

Marsden, George, *Reforming Fundamentalism: Fuller Seminary and the New Evangelicalism*. Michigan, Eerdmans, 1987.

Marsh, Simon, *A Voluntary Aided Church (of England) School*. Christians in Education, 1992.

Martin, Charles, 'How Plural Can You Get?', *Spectrum*, 1989, vol. 21:2, pages 145–72.

McCarthy, Rockne, *et al.*, *Society, State and Schools*. Michigan, Eerdmans, 1981.

McLaughlin, Terry, 'Christian Education and Schooling: A Liberal Perspective'. Unpublished paper, read at Stapleford House, 4 January, 1992a.

——, 'Fairness, Controversiality and the Common School', *Spectrum*, 1992b, vol. 24:2, pages 105–18.

——, 'The Ethics of Separate Schools', in Leicester, M., and Taylor, M., eds., *Ethics, Ethnicity and Education*. Kogan Page, 1992c.

Meakin, Derek, 'The Justification of Religious Education', *BJRE*, 1979, vol. 2:2, pages 49–55.

Bibliography

——, 'The Justification of Religious Education Reconsidered', *BJRE*, 1988, vol. 10:2, pages 92–6.

Meijer, Wilna, 'Religious Education and Personal Identity: A Problem for the Humanities', *BJRE*, 1991, vol. 13:2, pages 89–94.

Mitchell, Basil, 'Theology and Falsification', in Flew, Antony, Mac-Intyre, Alasdair, eds., *New Essays in Philosophical Theology*. SCM Press, 1955.

Montefiore, Hugh, ed., *The Gospel and Contemporary Culture*. Mowbray, 1992.

Mouw, Richard, and, Griffioen, Sander, *Pluralisms and Horizons*. Michigan, Eerdmans, 1993.

National Curriculum Council, *Analysis of LEA Agreed Syllabuses*, 1993.

Neill, Stephen, 'Religion and Culture—A Historical Introduction', in Stott, John and Coote, Robert, eds., *Down to Earth: Studies in Christianity and Culture*. Hodder & Stoughton, 1980.

Nelson, Ronald, 'Faith-Discipline Integration: Compatibilist, Reconstructionalist and Transformationalist Strategies', in Heie, Harold, and Wolfe, David, eds., *The Reality of Christian Learning*. Michigan, Eerdmans, 1987.

Netland, Harold, *Dissonant Voices: Religious Pluralism and the Question of Truth*. Apollos, 1991.

Neuhaus, John, ed., *Democracy and the Renewal of Public Education*. Michigan, Eerdmans, 1987.

Newbigin, Lesslie, *Foolishness to the Greeks*. SPCK, 1986.

——, *The Gospel in a Pluralist Society*. SPCK, 1989.

——, *Truth To Tell*. SPCK, 1991.

Nicholls, Bruce, 'Towards A Theology of Gospel and Culture', in Stott, John, and Coote, Robert, eds., *Down to Earth: Studies in Christianity and Culture*. Hodder & Stoughton, 1980.

——, 'Reflections on Canberra 1991', *World Evangelical Fellowship Theological News*, 1991, vol. 22:1, pages 4–5.

O'Keeffe, Bernadette, *Faith, Culture and the Dual System*. Falmer Press, 1986.

——, 'A Look at the Christian Schools Movement', in Watson, Brenda, ed., *Priorities in Religious Education*. Falmer Press, 1992.

Oldfield, Ken, 'Including Jainism', *BJRE*, 1986, vol. 8:3, pages 176–81.

Padilla, René, 'Hermeneutics and Culture—A Theological Perspective', in Stott, John, and Coote, Robert, eds., *Down to Earth: Studies in Christianity and Culture*. Hodder & Stoughton, 1980.

Palmer, Martin, *What Should We Teach?: Christians and Education in a Pluralist World*. Geneva, World Council of Churches, 1991.

Pascall, David, *Standards in Religious Education*. AREAI, 10 July, 1992.

Bibliography

Perks, Stephen, *The Christian Philosophy of Education Explained*. Avant Books, 1992.

Phillips, D. Z., *Faith After Foundationalism*. Routledge, 1988.

Phillips-Bell, M., 'Multi-cultural Education: A Critique of Walkling and Zec', *JPE*, 1981, vol. 15:1, pages 97–105.

Plantinga, Alvin, 'On Reformed Epistemology', in *The Reformed Journal*, January, 1982, vol. 32, pages 13–17.

——, 'Reason and Belief in God', in Plantinga, Alvin, and Wolterstorff, Nicholas, eds., *Faith and Rationality*. University of Notre Dame Press, 1983.

——, 'Epistemic Justification', *Nous*, 1986a, vol. 20, pages 3–18.

——, 'The Foundations of Theism: A Reply', *Faith and Philosophy*, 1986b, vol. 3:3, pages 298–313.

Polanyi, Michael, *Personal Knowledge*. Routledge & Kegan Paul, 1962.

——, *The Tacit Dimension*. Routledge & Kegan Paul, 1967.

Popper, Karl, *Conjectures and Refutations*. Routledge & Kegan Paul, 1963.

Race, Alan, *Christians and Religious Pluralism*. SCM Press, 1983.

Read, Garth, *et al.*, *How Do I Teach R.E.?* 2nd edn, Mary Glasgow Publications, 1992.

Roques, Mark, *Curriculum Unmasked*. Monarch/Christians in Education, 1989.

Rosenak, Julia, 'Should Children Be Subject to Paternalistic Restrictions on Their Liberties?', *JPE*, 1982, vol. 16:1, pages 89–96.

Runzo, Joseph, *Reason, Relativism and God*. MacMillan, 1986.

——, 'God, Commitment and Other Faiths: Pluralism versus Relativism', *Faith and Philosophy*, 1988, vol. 5:4, pages 343–64.

Russell, Richard, *Reason and Commitment in Education*. Unpublished M.Ed. thesis, University of Bristol, nd.

Schaeffer, Francis, *Escape From Reason*. InterVarsity Press, 1968a.

——, *The God Who Is There*. Hodder & Stoughton, 1968b.

——, *He Is There and He Is Not Silent*. Hodder & Stoughton, 1972.

——, *Genesis In Space and Time*. Hodder & Stoughton, 1973.

——, *The Great Evangelical Disaster*. Kingsway, 1984.

School Curriculum and Assessment Authority, *Model Syllabuses for Religious Education Consultation Document: Introduction*. SCAA, 1994.

Scottish Office Education Department, *Religious and Moral Education 5–14*. Scottish Office Education Department, 1992.

Scott, Drusilla, *Everyman Revisited*. Book Guild, 1985.

Shortt, John, 'A Critical Problem for Rational Autonomy', *Spectrum*, 1986, vol. 18:2, pages 107–21.

Skillen, James, *The Scattered Voice: Christians at Odds in the Public Square*. Michigan, Zondervan, 1990.

Storkey, Alan, *A Christian Social Perspective*. InterVarsity Press, 1979.

Storkey, Elaine, 'Change and Decay in British Society', in Eden, Martyn, and Wells, David, eds., *The Gospel in the Modern World*. InterVarsity Press, 1991.

Stott, John, and Coote, Robert, eds., *Down to Earth: Studies in Christianity and Culture*. Hodder & Stoughton, 1980.

Stott, John, *Issues Facing Christians Today*. Marshall, Morgan and Scott, 1984.

Sugden, Chris, 'Evangelicals and Religious Pluralism', in Hamnet, Ian, ed., *Religious Pluralism and Unbelief*. Routledge, 1990.

Swann, Lord, *Education For All*. HMSO, 1985.

Telegraph and Argus, 'Lessons in Agreement', 17 July, 1993.

Thatcher, Adrian, 'Learning to Become Persons: a theological approach to educational aims', in Francis, Leslie, and Thatcher Adrian, eds., *Christian Perspectives For Education*. Gracewing, 1990.

Thiessen, Elmer, 'Religious Freedom and Educational Pluralism', in Manley-Casmir, Michael, ed., *Family Choice In Schooling*. Massachusets, Lexington Books, 1982.

——, 'A Defense of a Distinctively Christian Curriculum', *Religious Education*, 1985, vol. 80:1, pages 37–50.

——, 'Two Concepts or Two Phases of Education', *JPE*, 1987, vol. 21:2, pages 223–34.

——, 'Christian Nurture, Indoctrination and Liberal Education', *Spectrum*, 1991, vol. 23:2, pages 105–24.

——, *Teaching for Commitment*. Gracewing, 1993.

Tluanga, L. N., *Teacher's Challenge*. New Delhi, Interserve, 1989.

Totterdell, Michael, 'Understanding Religion: The Landscape and the Quest'. Unpublished MA thesis, University of London, 1988.

Trigg, Roger, *Reality At Risk*. Harvester Press, 1980.

Van Til, Cornelius, *In Defense of the Faith: A Survey of Christian Epistemology*. Phillipsburg, New Jersey, Presbyterian & Reformed Publishing, 1932.

——, *A Christian Theory of Knowledge*. Phillipsburg, New Jersey, Presbyterian & Reformed Publishing Company, 1969.

——, *Essays on Christian Education*. Nutley, New Jersey, Presbyterian & Reformed Publishing, 1971.

——, *In Defense of the Faith: Christian Theistic Evidences*. Phillipsburg, New Jersey, Presbyterian & Reformed Publishing, 1976.

——, *Apologetics*. Phillipsburg, New Jersey, Presbyterian & Reformed Publishing, 1980.

Walsh, Brian, and Middleton, Richard, *The Transforming Vision*. Downers Grove, USA, InterVarsity Press, 1984.

Watson, Brenda, *Education and Belief*. Basil Blackwell, 1987.

Watts, Andrew, 'Some Biblical Perspectives on Schooling', *Spectrum*, 1992, vol. 24:1, pages 53–62.

Westhill College, *Distance Learning in RE: Prospectus*. Newman and Westhill Colleges, nd.

White, John, *Towards A Compulsory Curriculum*. Routledge & Kegan Paul, 1973.

Wilson, John, 'First Steps in Religious Education', in Watson, Brenda, ed., *Priorities in Religious Education*. Falmer Press, 1992.

Wolters, Albert, *Creation Regained*. InterVarsity Press, 1985.

Wolterstorff, Nicholas, 'Is Reason Enough?', *The Reformed Journal*, April 1981, vol. 31, pages 20–4.

——, 'Introduction', in Plantinga, Alvin, and Wolterstorff, Nicholas, eds., *Faith and Rationality*. University of Notre Dame Press, 1983a.

——, 'Can Belief in God Be Rational If It Has No Foundations?', in Plantinga, Alvin, and Wolterstorff, Nicholas, eds., *Faith and Rationality*. University of Notre Dame Press, 1983b.

——, *Reason Within the Bounds of Religion*. Michigan, Eerdmans, 1984.

Wright, Christopher, 'The Authority of Scripture in an Age of Relativism: Old Testament Perspectives', in Eden, Martyn, and Wells, David, eds., *The Gospel in the Modern World*. InterVarsity Press, 1991.

——, 'Editorial: P for Pentateuch, Patriarchs and Pagans', *Themelios*, 1993, vol. 18:2, pages 3–4.

Index

Index

Index